STOP MAJORING IN THE MINORS

The Thinking Approach On How To Create The Life You
Want Rather Than
Tolerating The Life You Have

Brandon L. Draper

DEDICATION

This book is dedicated to my Mother & Father Elizabeth & Floyd Draper. To all my love ones Family and Friends that have stood tall during all the trials and tribulations!

Brandon L. Draper

"The Motivational King"

Free Training Videos

This book includes some how-to videos and interviews about the writing process and book publishing that can help you and your business benefit, from getting new clients, closing more sales and obtaining speaking engagements.

Go here: http://bit.ly/2S7nlTL

Disclaimer

I want to help you survive and thrive. Having said that, I'm not a doctor or a clinical therapist. I don't play one on the Internet or on TV, so consult a license professional or doctor for any mental or health advice. Please seek medical supervision before attempting to do anything recommended in this book. If there's a tiebreaker to be made, don't listen to me. Trust your instincts.

Don't do anything stupid with yours or someone else's life.

AKNOWLEDGEMENT

I would like to begin by thanking God; without whom, I don't think I would have amassed to anything today. My profound gratitude goes to my amiable mother; Elizabeth C. Draper and my very intelligent, witty stuck-in-his-way father, Floyd Draper for availing themselves as vessels through which I came to the world and giving me the opportunity to be in a position where I can share my thoughts and ideas with the world! I want to truly thank everybody who took the time to give me a few words of kindness or guidance.

I remember when I was at my lowest ebb, or so it felt, in this world. You came and showed me love as if I was your child and never uttered a word of discouragement. A special thanks goes to Raymond Smith, I am forever indebted to you, I can never repay everything you have done for me in five lifetimes; you have been immense.

Special thanks goes to my wonderful, supportive friends Wandy Ortega, Damien Young & Manson Miller who tolerated my long but informed dialogues about business, history, spirituality, and public affairs, you were the reason this book is a finished work today.

To all who have contributed to the achievement of this great success, time and space will not allow me to mention your names one after the other. Your efforts were really appreciated and duly acknowledged.

CONTENTS

1

CHAPTER ONE

WHAT WORRIES YOU AT NIGHT KEEPS YOU LOSING IN LIFE

Worrying is like a rocking chair; it gives you something to do,
but it gets you nowhere.

-Glenn Turner

I hope you are ready for the journey we're about to embark on because it will be an interesting one. Most people spend their entire lives worrying about things that will never happen.

They waste their strengths on things they cannot change, things that only exist in their wildest imagination, thus, staying awake all through the night.

What happens in their imagination can be likened to a million things of the worst nature happening at the same time. If you are part of the people who take their time to focus on the negative things in life and believe they will happen to them, you will surely not get far in your race to success.

What worries you at night keeps you from moving in life. What exactly does that mean? These are things that you fear the most, they are things that compete for your attention and make you concentrate less on things that really matter. For example, you may spend the whole night thinking about how likely you are to lose your job. This thought may go on in your mind causing you to forget about carrying out your duties at work. Instead of you taking a proactive approach and figuring out what ways you can bring the situation under control, you may end up worsening the whole scenario and become stranded when your fear finally materializes. If you feel you are going to lose your job, it will be more sensible to worry about your survival when the thought materializes than worrying about the thought itself.

Now, one of the most common fears, I believe, is poverty. Everyone is scared at the mere thought of poverty. No one wants to lose everything that they have and no one, for the most part, wants to live on the street and not have the necessities of life. It is fear that will keep you up at night. Just because you're worried about your children, worried about how your family will survive, worried about losing the shelter you have, nursing such worries will end up making you lose out on life's best moments.

By life, I am referring to your goals and dreams. Instead of nursing the fears and believing in the situations it brings your way, I would suggest that you focus on finding other avenues that can help you get a better grasp of what you need to do in your life in order to take your life to the next level and be able to get the career you want.

We're always in this heightened, alert phase where we hold the opinion that we can never elevate our thinking past our current situation. The fear becomes about something that most likely won't happen. Instead, we should take a proactive approach and figure out how to put ourselves in positions that will enable us to move to the next level, elevate our thinking and subsequently alleviate our fear.

Right now, our current situation spells potential disaster. Now, the disaster we see in our mind, in our imagination, may seem imminent when it's truly far. But we live in the present.

So, the present, in our minds, is in direct proportion to what's going to happen next, or what we fear will be manifested next. When that happens, we must take a brief pause and realize that what we're most afraid of is controlling our lives. And when we limit ourselves this way through fear, our maximum capability is limited. We can be in denial and hold the cliched point of view that fear is nothing but false evidence appearing real. But the truth is that, in our mind, we are manifesting true fear.

Such fears come in different categories and dimension. They may manifest in the form of; the fear of being poor, the fear of losing everything, the fear of embarrassment, the fear of people looking at us as if we're inadequate. Those are legitimate fears that we internalize.

We can say that you don't need to think on the positive side, but our mind is designed to protect itself. So, for us to possibly put ourselves in a position to protect ourselves, our mind has a tendency of thinking of or dwelling on things that need to be addressed.

The problem that comes with that is the mind subconsciously puts those things before us and tells us this is what we need to be concerned about. Our conscious mind keeps reminding us of the need to look at the situation and put ourselves in a position to decide to act, to change the possible conflict within ourselves. We can say let's change the way you're thinking. Well, the way that we're thinking is in direct relation to the way that we are reacting, or should I say, the way that we are responding to our outside external factors.

Our thinking has a lot to do with the way we decide to live our lives. The more severed our thinking ability, the more scattered and disorganized our entire life would be.

We must change our manner of response to external factors if we're ultimately going to change the way we think, because we can't trick ourselves to believe something when we don't see it manifesting. When we're looking at the great scope of what's really going on, we have a fear of something because the way we're responding or reacting to it, those are two different things.

If you are reacting to something, it has a tendency of having a negative connotation. Why? Because we are waiting for something to happen and then reacting to it versus having a response, which means we're more proactive.

Think about it for a second. If you go to the doctor and they prescribe some medication to you and that medication has a negative reaction, it means that your body didn't respond to it well; hence, the reaction. You're breaking out in hives; it's negative. If they give the same medication to you and now you have a positive response, it did not elicit any negative effects on you.

We really need to train our minds to be proactive rather than reactive. Only a proactive mind can confidently source out solutions to the issues going on in the mind. A reactive mind will simply act on what is being thought of and influence the body into carrying out the task. There is a great power behind how our mind operates.

It's the same thing in the world of understanding how the mind works; how it relates to fear and how it can ultimately derail you from getting to a point in life that you need to be. Rather than allowing the mind to act upon the fear and taking a proactive approach, you wait until there needs to be a reaction to it, meaning, you have lost what you've got, and have absolutely nothing else to fall back on.

Now that you're in a bad situation, you must react. Now, you must go on the resources that you did not have because you didn't properly prepare. So now, all those nights you spent staying up mean nothing. You didn't get ahead from doing it. In fact, you're further behind than you were initially because you're tired and drained.

But you are still yet to perform, and you must perform no matter what, keeping in mind that how you perform means everything.

Your performance is directly proportional to how prepared your mind is. The question then comes in, "how did you prepare for the situation?" Well, I prepare for the situation by worrying about it. I stayed up late at night worrying about it.

So, did you do anything proactive? Did you take any actions? Did you attempt to look for another career? Did you attempt to start a business that could ultimately replace what you're doing?

Now, when I say a business or career, I mean something that truly fulfills you. Because, at the end of the day, just doing something, simply to get by, is, going to ensure that life gets by you since you're not doing something you love.

Doing something you really love tends to improve your mind's engagement into the whole activity and you may have something to fall back on when the stress kicks in.

There's a saying that goes to the effect of when you do something you love, you never have to work a day in your life. But when you don't have a love for it, and you're just doing it for its sake, what fulfillment do you receive? What purpose do you have in doing it?

If a janitor is mopping the floor, he may have a "WHY" that's much deeper than what you or I may understand it to be. We may never understand his "why", but he takes pride in what he does because it means something to him.

It could be a generational thing, where his father and his mother, or someone that he knows and holds in high regard, did domestic work and because he values such, he begins to see it as something that he wants.

In one way or the other, he has found a way to relate with that work and derive joy from it. I once came across a little girl who wanted to become a teacher. She wanted to teach children in the same manner she saw her mom doing at work.

It may not be what you and I want in our lives, but in his value system that's what he wants. And guess what? He's not wrong, because that's what he wants, and that's what fulfills him. Only what you cherish can make you fulfilled. To understand your purpose is everything.

It has absolutely nothing to do with anyone else, because your purpose is unique to yourself, and your purpose is self- defined by what has been given to you from the heavens. It's been pre-destined for you to have that attribute within yourself. No one can define that for you, other than yourself. Does it make you happy? Do you feel fulfilled, instead of just worrying about things that are not under your control?

You can't control anybody else or any situation out there, other than yourself and the situation within you. What you will figure out real soon is, as soon as you're able to control what's going on inside of you, you can control a lot more of what's going on even on the outside.

You must master yourself before you can master anything else, and the first thing you have to master is your thoughts. If you understand how to master your thoughts, your thoughts are ultimately going to be able to control the way you feel, and the way you feel will control the things you do.

Instead of worrying about things at night, because those things at night are going to keep you away from having the things you want in life, because you'll always be hesitant to move forward because of a fear that you have in your mind; this means you must stop worrying in order to have the things you want in your life.

You must master your thoughts. You must master your thought in order to take your life to the next level. We're at a point now where, we see what we need to do, and how we need to address it. Where do we go from here?

It's simple! We must condition our mind. A lot of people out there will say "that's hard to do". What I want you to gather from this text is to have a conversation with yourself.

Have an honest conversation with yourself to come to the realization of figuring out what it is that you really want from this world. Is it just to survive? Is it to really thrive? What is it that you really and truly want? What is it in this world that defines who you are and embodies your values and morals?

It's easy for us to look at other people and try to emulate something that we're truly not. But to be unique, and to be one with yourself, it alleviates a lot of these symptoms of fear that are direct proportions of what someone else fears due to the way their life is built.

But when you build your life in a certain way, there are things that you don't have to worry about. There are things that you don't have to fear. So, how we identify ourselves determines our destiny. And how we identify ourselves is dependent upon how we think of ourselves; not how others receive us; not how others think about us, but how we perceive and see ourselves in our minds, and the potential we have for ourselves.

How do we see that potential? No matter what accomplishment you have or don't have; no matter how much education you have or don't have; if you believe you can do anything, then you can surely do it.

Once our mind can conceive it, our bodies will surely act on it. Now that's not a motivational fluff. It is conditioning your mindset. That's the law of attraction concerning how we think. Because whatever a man thinks, so he becomes.

Whatever a man sees, is what he gets. You are a direct product of your thoughts.

If you believe that you can do it, then you can manifest it in your life; Law of attraction. There are countless times in history where we have seen people lacking in education and resources rising and attaining the level of education they aspired toward.

They wanted to transform this world, they wanted to transform some ideology in life, and they were able to do it when all the odds were stacked against them.

I challenge you today, to take a whole new approach to your life, adopt an outlook where you are starting to respond to life and not react to it. Make proactive moves to take control so you can get rid of that symptom of fear in your life. And then you can begin to start acting on life. And I hope you gathered this information from this chapter to take your life to the next level. To transform and transcend you to another level of understanding of how you're going to live a much positive life.

BRIDGE

She hadn't been able to sleep in a month. Sleep seemed like a luxury now. Each time she closed her eyes to sleep, Georgina Davis dreamt of shadows pursuing her. Slowly, she sat up, turned on her bedside lamp and sighed.

"How in the hell did I get myself into this mess?" She asked out loud.

She had no answer for her question. Slowly, like a little girl, Gina spared a glance at the bedside clock and cursed. The time was 2am. She had been lying in her bed for over two hours, thinking of the fact that she may lose everything she had struggled to achieve within the twinkle of an eye.

"Damn it!" She exclaimed once again.

Gina swung her long slim legs on the marble floor. She went on her feet and dejectedly walked to the dressing table near her closet. She took a good look at herself in the dressing mirror. At thirty, she looked twenty-five. Her thick red curly hair was in disarray. She pushed back a strand of hair that was dangling against her cheek. She had a pair of violet eyes that sparkle when she got angry. Her nose was long and pointed. She had a pair of pink, full and luscious lips. Her high aristocratic cheekbones were pale. She had a long neck.

She was tall, almost too tall for a lady. Her breasts were small, full and firm. Gina stared down at her flat stomach, her slim waist and down her long legs. Her hips went well with her slim structure.

The thing was, she had been considered a beauty from the age of five. She knew she was beautiful. Men of all ages stared down at her when she walked pass them or when she talked. Today, Gina's beauty was the last thing on her mind. She had other important things to think of.

She was about to lose her job and Gina had been so troubled by this that sleep had been eluding her. She spied a few lines beneath her eyes, and she knew that she couldn't cheat on nature for so long.

Sooner or later, she would collapse.

"My career is about to go down the drain." She groaned again.

Oh yes, her world was crashing in around her. A single mistake was about to cost her career and she didn't know how she would cope with her kids' school fees, food, and other basic needs.

Gina was an accountant with the glamorous IT firm. As the head accountant, she was responsible for recording the flow of money in the firm. She was responsible for monitoring the flow of money in the firm. Unknowingly for her, her assistant had been laundering money. Only she and Carl, her assistant had the password to her computer. Gina had trusted Carl so much that his betrayal was never expected.

"My problem is that I trust too much." She muttered.

Her manager, Jack had walked into her office a month ago and demanded she explained the disappearance of twenty thousand dollars from the company's account.

Gina had stared at the man as if he was insane. "Surely sir, there must be a mistake." She supplied.

"Of course, there's a problem, twenty thousand dollars is missing under your watch. How in the hell will you explain this?"

He had stormed out of the office. With shaking hands, Gina clicked on her computer and began to dig. Five minutes later, two auditors appeared. They had been sent by Jack. After two hours of intense investigation, it was discovered that twenty thousand dollars was indeed missing.

"You have to believe me, I know nothing about this." She tried to explain.

"You are the head accountant. Only you have the password for..." The auditors said.

"Yes, but Carl also has the password to my computer." She explained.

Carl was summoned for a meeting the following day. He never appeared. He had disappeared. The case was still being investigated and she had been on suspension.

"My career is about to go down the drain and I can do nothing about it."

Gina knew that soon; the investigation would be over. The firm would insist she pay the stolen money and twenty thousand dollars was not twenty dollars. No one would hire her if she had been accused of fraud.

"How would I explain to my kids that our lives are about to take another turn?"

Amy was ten and Turner was seven. Gina had always thrived to give her kids the best life could offer. She may not only lose her job she may also lose her life savings.

The thought of falling from grace to grass made her almost weep with sadness. Gina had grown up in poverty and she had worked night and day to reach her current position. In a few weeks, Carl had succeeded in tarnishing her image. When she gets sacked, no one would ever hire her again.

Since Gina worried so much at night, she hardly ate nor even laugh. She had succeeded in fooling the kids, but she knew she couldn't fool them any longer. She hated the fact that she spent more time worrying and not thinking of a way forward.

"You have to plan ahead." She told herself

Gina sat on the dressing chair. She came to the realization that her career in accounting may be over already. But she was also an event planner. All she needed to do was get the capital towards opening her own business.

Thinking and worrying without doing anything would only destroy her. She had kids to fend for and she had her hands to work with.

"The worst that could happen is to lose my job."

When this happened, she could switch career and move to event planning and decoration. Fearing the fact that she was a disgrace and that her career was over would do her no good.

Gina vowed it was time she stopped worrying and start thinking of a way forward

Gina smiled genuinely for the first time in a month. She climbed into bed and within ten minutes, she was sleeping soundlessly.

2

CHAPTER TWO

DOUBLING YOUR WORTH IS NOT A CURSE

Your positive action combined with positive thinking results in success.

-Shiv Khera

In this chapter, we shall be focusing on how to get rid of self-defeating thoughts and ideas. And one of the ways that we're going to do that is to talk about how "doubling your worth is not a curse." What exactly does that mean? It means that, for most people, they associate wealth with evil or wickedness. You want to be a person of wealth. Whether that's money, or knowledge, independence, resources, reliability, it doesn't matter as long

as its wealth.

Now, if you're able to double your worth and not perceive it as a curse; that is, not considering having more than others something bad. Well, that was years ago, and I showed an example before in one of my books, I was working for a company when I was in college. And one of the things the CEO explained to me while I was in this company, a failed company in the mortgage industry. And he explained to me, he said, "the only thing that you can do for poor people is not to become one of them." And a part of me after hearing this really got angered because I had a heart for those that had less. I wanted to help them because, if I looked back at my childhood, I didn't have it all, but don't get misconstrued, I had a meal every day and I always had a place to stay but we weren't wealthy, and we weren't rich. When I saw people who were poor, I had a heart for them, and I always wanted to help. I always felt pity for them and there is a part of me that always wants to reach out to them.

When this gentleman said this, I looked at him differently in a way because he was a mentor to me. And I thought he was just a bit out of touch with reality and what's going on. It took me a couple of days and I finally approached him about it. I said, "that comment, I really look up to you and I really respect you, but that comment you made really made me feel some type of way because I feel as if you're out of touch with what's going on in our community.

" He looked at me for a long time. And in that moment, he was really thinking hard about what he was going to say to me. But what he said to me was very simple.

He said, "in order for you to use someone that is lesser in the world, someone that's poor, the only way that you are able to help that person is to not become one of them". He went on to say, "because, if you are that person you're trying to help, how then can you help? But if you are the opposite of who you are trying to help, then you can help to elevate them to where you're at. You can never give out what you don't have. You can't help the poor by being poor. You can't bring them out of their pains and agony by living on their level. Only a man above can bring someone up."

Those words have never left my mind; that, in order to help someone, often, you must be elevated over that person.

Now, some may agree, and some may disagree with me; but, if two people are struggling with the same thing, it'll be harder to take the other out of the situation because the same

situation you suffer from is what I suffer from. We can share a good conversation, but is anything else going to move for the other person than a great conversation? That's one of the pivotal things I've learned earlier on. However, understand that you must put yourself in a position to double your worth in whatever it is that you decide you want to invest in.

You decide whatever that investment is going to be, not me. What are you going to invest in? Is its personal development? Wealth creation? Style and sophistication? Acquisition of a new skill? Learning another language so that you can speak to others of different dialects? What is it that you are willing to invest in? You need to double your worth in whatever it is you want to invest in, and you need to do so with the understanding that, it is not a curse.

Now, let's go into the money, because that's the main facet of what most people probably want to read about in this book anyway. What do I mean by doubling your worth is not a curse? It means, you can come up with a systematic way of taking control of money through investments and through real estate and through different business ventures so that when you leave, you're able to pass everything on to the next person coming along. Understand this: A lot of people will say, when I leave here, I'm not trying to make anyone rich, and I understand that. But here's a thought, why are you here if none of what you have belongs to you?

It's just a loan because what adorns you one day will adorn another next. You cannot put value into jewelry and to clothes and the cars because as soon as you leave, someone

else will be driving your car, wearing your jewelry, and living in your house. The bottom-line is this; don't take value to things that are not even yours.

I have never seen a house, or a double-wide trailer being towed to a graveyard. You don't take those things with you but understand why you're here. You need to double what it is that doubles your value. Because if you double your value, you're doubling your legacy, because there are people, i.e. your family members, that ultimately depend on you. What you're ultimately doing is leaving a blueprint on how to do what you did, but a whole lot faster. That's why you want to double.

You want to be ten times your efforts so that each generation will remember your name, now you're able to leave a blueprint on how to do it. There are multiple times in history if you can recount, that people, families, have created a certain amount of wealth. The Rockefellers, Bill Gates, Mark Zuckerberg and all these other individuals, and what we see is that they have created an enormous amount of wealth in a short period of time.

Was it about them just creating this in a short period of time, or were there principles instilled in them over time, such that when the opportunity came, they were able to excel? That goes back to "what is the definition of success?" The definition of success is when opportunity meets preparation.

Preparation meets opportunity, can be translated as when you are prepared and an opportunity comes along, you're going to be successful. But if the opportunity comes and you're not prepared, you will not be successful. If you look at all these situations or all these famous, rich, wealthy people, they were prepared over the years through education, through family experiences, through the passing of financial principles down from succeeding generations until the opportunity came that allowed those principles and those strategies to be leveraged upon. Then, they catapulted.

So, is it wrong to double your worth? No, it's not. Because, you're going to make it easier for future generations. You're going to make it easier for other pioneers and entrepreneurs to come and be able to capitalize off what you have started. Now that we've gone past this is not a curse, let's talk about the importance of doing it and how that works. Now, how do you do it?

Understand this, what is the equalizer of all the qualities? It is the amount of time we all have. I don't care how much billions of dollars you have, I don't care how much power any individual has. The one thing that's guaranteed is that there are 24 hours in a day.

That is the grand equalizer. The second equalizer is that no matter how rich or how poor you are, as sure as you were born, you shall die. Those are the equalizers. Time is the only certainty in the life of man, every other thing is uncertain and comes into being by chance.

Now, the only sense of that part is, if you have a little bit more money, you may be able to prolong your longevity, but at the end of the day, you're going to leave here one way or the other. 24 hours is the equalizer, meaning whatever it is that Bill Gates or Mark Zuckerberg or Oprah Winfrey are doing in their 24 hours for the last 20, 30 years, you may not have been doing in your 24 hours for the last 20, 30 years, and that's why your bank account is in different proportions across the board.

Your investments are in different proportions across the board. We see their wealth and what they have been able to amount to over the years, and you say well why I can't be that. Or, they were lucky or had a great opportunity.

Donald Trump in one of his interviews, and one thing that I really, really took from him, He said, "I don't believe in luck. What I've found is the harder I work, the luckier I am." Think about luck and how directly that is with work ethic. If you want to double your worth, you want to quadruple your worth, how much are you willing to work within those 24 hours, because we all have 24 hours.

What are we going to do with our 24 hours that's different than what the other person is doing in their 24 hours? We want to emulate some of what they have, meaning that -- I don't believe I'm in competition with anyone, so I'm very cognizant of not wanting what another man has, or another woman has.

I may lack a certain lifestyle and want that for myself to have personal freedom and to be able to have the type of wealth to be able to do things I enjoy for me, not for them

and what they're doing, but for me. You've got to oftentimes think about this too, when you're trying to double your wealth, what are you willing to pay in order to have what they have.

There may be some things that you may have to go through to have that. Are you willing to pay the ticket? If you're not willing to pay the ticket, stop stressing yourself out as if you're going to do something you know ultimately you will not.

That will drive you crazy, and we don't want you to go crazy, we want you to get the truth here and understand to dismiss all the myths about creating money, creating wealth. All those things are simple. It's not complicated, it's very simple.

Once we dismiss all that stuff and you come to the realization that if you sit down and come up with a strategy, a concrete solid, simple, plan. It's the dignity of simplicity that makes everything operate in harmony. It's not the complicated in the world, it's the dignity of simplicity.

We know that it is not a curse. Now what? What do we do? What's the major thing that we can do now? Well, how do we take control? We can look at what other people are doing successfully, secretly.

So now we can read books, we can educate and go to seminars, we can get associations going on. When I say associations, meaning that we hang around people that we want their lifestyle. So, we understand that there's a process to

follow to get to that level of success. And that's guaranteed. But the question is, are you listening?

I've read a lot of books that I never quite understood how someone can struggle through a situation for 10 years plus, when there are books that have been written about the issues that they are struggling with, and it could really give them the knowledge to help with the situation at hand.

You can learn how to get past that problem, quite literally, in a weekend. Yet, no one reads the book, no one listens to the message. That's strange and I just don't quite understand it. As a result, when I write my books, I try to write in a way that helps everyone to understand these principles in the simplest of ways. I believe in dignity and simplicity. If you make it simple, you will connect with a lot of people.

We don't have to get into all these complicated, minutia. It simply confuses people. Let's talk about the basics, because you understand--If you can learn the basics of something, and you keep on repeating it over and over and over, no matter how bad you are, eventually, you will become average at the minimum. If you become average, eventually you will become good; if you become good, you'll eventually become great. Then eventually, you will want to aspire to be one of the greatest. But it takes practice. Take the simple things and just keep on repeating it until you're a master.

In the military, we call it battle drills. You see, doing something over and over and over, until it becomes second nature to you. We understand now that we are equal, in essence, we all have 24 hours to get any given thing accomplished.

If we all have 24 hours, what are we doing? Who are we surrounding ourselves with? What resources are we putting in place in those 24 hours to be able to capitalize and be able to take our life, our business, everything, to the next level?

These questions are what make the difference.

The question you ought to be asking right now is "now that I have this information, how do I use it?' Because getting your hands-on information doesn't make your enlightened, unless you act on it, what you have acquired can never metamorphose into what you desire.

The energy we acquire from gathering information is simply 'potential'. How do we turn that energy of knowing, into kinetic, to actual action and application?

I know the rule of how this works. I know that I can have it just like anyone else, despite my lack of other resources. Despite my lack of education, I know I can have it no matter what. I know that I can double my worth because I understand it's not a curse.

Basically, that's why you've never obtained success. That's why you've never obtained the wealth that you wanted to be in your life. Because you just felt like it was a curse. It was negative. Now, why did you think it was something negative? Well, simply, because that what you've been conditioned to believe.

If you believe that something's negative, it's almost like a bottle of poison with the skull and crossed bones label on it. That means stay away, it will kill you. If you see something, a curse, it's like poison, then you stay away from it. What you've been conditioned to believe is, poison is destructive, but the truth is that, it is the complete opposite. It's life- changing. It's building.

There's nothing that you can do more when you become a wealthy person, whether in heart, soul, spirit, or monetarily, you have an overabundance of something that you can share, because that's what this life is about, giving and sharing.

If you're able to share with someone something that you have in overabundance, wouldn't that add value to your life? Wouldn't that double your worth? Because you're able to share and give people experiences.

There are a lot of people that may not have doubled their worth monetarily, but they've doubled their worth ethically, morally, and values. These people, when they pass from time to eternity I mean, it literally took so much time in the present to have this ceremony complete because something in people were touched by the worth that they presented in the world.

This doesn't have to be monetarily. It is about the values, and morals, and what they stood for that doubled, I mean, quadrupled their worth on Earth. You must take that into

consideration that you've been conditioned to think a way. Now, you must condition yourself to know that what you

once know was a curse to you -- an example of that is simple. You see a father and a son at a sink and the father is shaving his beards with a razor.

The son is looking at him in the light. If that father was to mistakenly walk out of that bathroom and leave that razor on the counter and that son was to pick that razor up and scrape his face in the same fashion that his father did, it would cut his face up. What he sees now that fascinates him at that moment is a curse to him, but with the right knowledge and the right maturity in the present, it will turn out to be a blessing to him. The thing about it is this, we must be conditioned.

We must have the right education because if we think that something's a curse and that's the way our mind is built around it, and we still go against our nature of what we've been taught and conditioned to believe, and then go against it, there's a tendency to self-destruct.

Like a thermostat, it's not going to go past 70 because that's where it's been set to. Even when you go after something, but deep down inside, your nature tells you to go against it, doing so will only result in self-sabotaging.

This is the problem with that type of thinking. Now, you must condition yourself to think differently, to change your nature and how it relates to it. When you go after that which you want and make steps. Instead of self-sabotaging, start setting yourself up for success.

BRIDGE

Her alarm went off at exactly 6am. She slowly opened her eyes and then smiled. She was happy with the honest

decision she had made with herself. Finally, she wouldn't live her life in fear again. She was determined to double her worth and working towards it was now her goal.

She jumped from the bed and stretched her limbs.

"It sure would be a beautiful day." Gina prophesied with a smile on her beautiful face.

She picked a robe and donned it over her short nighty. Within minutes, Gina was out of the door. Her first stop was Amy's room.

She gave the door a rap.

"Sweetie you're going to be late for school." She said quietly.

Without thinking, Gina pushed the door opened and found her daughter lying on her stomach.

"Sweetie…" She called again.

"Can't I stay back home today?" Amy pouted.

"No sweetie. You have to bath, eat and then go to school." She sat on her daughter's bed.

"But mom..." Amy began.

Gina caressed her daughter's face. Amy had her thick red hair while she had her late father's amber eyes.

"Young lady, you will get yourself out of your bed, shower, eat and go to school."

Amy burst out laughing. She jumped from her bed and ran to the bathroom. Gina smiled and walked out of her daughter's room. She opened the door to Turner's room and found him popped up against the pillows. Gina sat on the edge of the bed and gently patted his cheeks.

He smiled and burrowed closer to her.

"Sweetie, its morning already and you're going to be late for school."

Turner's eyes flew open. He smiled and then sat up.

"Miss Green would be taking us to see, "The sound of music." He said in an excited tone.

"Sweetie, you've seen that movie countless times." His mother reminded him.

"I don't care mom. I won't ever get tired of seeing that movie. You said it that you saw that movie countless times."

Gina let out a loud laugh.

"Come on darling, go have your bath. You don't want to miss the school bus, do you?"

"No mom."

Turner climbed down from the bed and dashed into the bathroom. Gina walked back to the kitchen. She stiffened a yawn and set about preparing breakfast of scrambled eggs, toast bread and tea.

As she prepared breakfast for the kids, Gina allowed her mind to wonder towards the steps she would need to take in order to double her worth. She would need capital, a shop, an online site, and complimentary cards. Above all, she would need market.

"Mom, have you seen my pen?" Amy asked from the door way.

"I think I saw a pen on the sofa in the living room."

Amy dashed to the living room while Gina served the kids. They sat down in the dining room and had breakfast. Turner kept chatting about the movie his class would be seeing later in the day. Amy kept playing with her phone.

"Mom?" Turner called. "Yes darling?"

"Why haven't you been going to work lately?" Gina took a deep breath.

"Actually, I am thinking of changing career. I want to go into event planning and decoration."

Amy immediately stared at her mother. "Why is that?"

Gina shrugged. "I'm having issues with my firm and its

time I look elsewhere."

"What do you mean?" Amy asked innocently.

"Don't worry your pretty little head Amy. I have everything under control."

She took a good look at the big clock on the wall and sighed.

"Come on kids, the school bus will be here any minute."

The kids pushed back their chairs. They picked their backpacks and kissed their mother goodbye.

As soon as the kids were gone, Gina returned to the living room. She picked a notepad and a biro. Without hesitation, Gina began to make plans for her new business. The only problem she would have now was capital.

Her cell phone rang, and she took it and then pressed the receiver button.

"Hello?"

"Miss Davis?" She heard John, her boss called. "Good morning John."

"Good morning Gina. I've sent you an email two days ago. Have you gone through it?"

"It has been days since I've checked my email."

"Please do. We can't wait to have you back." John told her with a smile.

Gina couldn't help but frown. She didn't understand what he meant.

"What do you mean?" "Just check your email."

He said and the line went dead. Gina settled back against the sofa. She went to her email and logged in. She had about a half of dozen emails. The one that got her attention was the one from her Boss. She clicked on it and read it.

"Hi Georgina, Carl had been arrested last week. He had confessed to have stolen the money without your knowledge. Can you come to the office and let's have a talk?"

Gina stared at the mail and tears of Joy slipped down her cheeks. She was happy that finally, her name had been cleared and her image had not been tarnished.

"The man couldn't even apologize for the emotional, psychological and physical trauma he had caused me."

Gina smiled and then laughed. Finally, she would have the capital she needed for her new business. She would go hunting for an office, she would need complimentary cards and then finally, she would open an online page to showcase her goods.

"Never will I go back to that firm again." She thought

out loud.

Finally, Gina was on her way to doubling her worth. Her employers had discarded her like a piece of clothing at the first sign of trouble. They had not even given her the benefit of a doubt. Never would she work for anyone again. She had worked for the glamorous IT firm for over six years, where had it taken her?

Today, a new dawn had started in her life. A new chapter had started, and Gina couldn't wait to start experiencing the sweetness of it all.

3

CHAPTER THREE

USE YOUR THINKING CAP OR IT'S A WRAP

Success is a lousy teacher. It seduces smart people into thinking they can't lose.

-Bill Gates

Think little goals and expect little achievements.
Think big goals and win big success.

-David Joseph Schwartz

One of the things that we've discovered through our studies of humanity is that most individuals do not think. This is a habit of humans for unknown reasons. The common man has succeeded in making his brain redundant and inactive for quite a very long time now. Most people will believe that they actually think for the most part in their life, and I'm not trying to delineate your educational level or your level of intelligence; but it's a proven fact that most people don't think. Earl Nightingale came up with "The Strangest Secret," where he systematically dove deep and spoke about how most men do not think. In this chapter, one of the things I want you to understand is that you must think. If you must rise above those you are interested in helping, then there is a need for your thoughts, only thinkers have the power to link problems with the right solutions.

You must put on your thinking cap otherwise, this means that you're going to lose out on so many opportunities in your personal life, business, profession, and whatever endeavor it is that you attempt to do. Because, if you're not involved in yourself with a systematic way on how to intake information and come up with a decision-making process to systematically know how to put things in the right order that's going to be advantageous to your success, your venture may turn out otherwise.

Now, there are countless times where we've seen kings and emperors and some of the most influential people in life make some very tough decisions, but they had to decide. This

decision didn't just come randomly off the top of their heads, they had to seek advice. They got advice on what they should do. They got advice on the right course of action and they thought about the process. Ever heard of the saying, "let me sleep on it."? Well, when they say sleep on it, what that really means is, let me think about it. It is quite uncommon to find a high office without a board that assists it to think. Before a kingdom or business empire can survive in this competitive world, advice and the ability to think cannot be undermined.

Give me time to internalize the information and be able to decipher what's really going on. Do I read-between-the- lines, and as a leader, be able to come out and make a clear, concise decision that's going to be advantageous for my organization, for my personal life, my business, or whatever the issue that you're dealing with? For you to be successful, you must put on your thinking cap.

If you do not put on your thinking cap, you're going to get your head cut off from the neck. In other words, you're going to give away some of the most vital information of your company. Your thinking cap is supposed to obtain and process data into information that can be useful to the entire body system at large.

You're going to give ideas away to your competition, or your competition is going to steal ideas from you. You're not going to know how to be able to face competition. You're not going to know how to address certain critical times where you're going to have to, as a leader, make critical decisions. Those decisions are going to have to be based off a sound

foundation of knowing how to move, when to move, and why you are moving in the direction that you are, and while this is on think about the longevity of the company, the business, or whatever you're doing. You always must maintain a level of thinking.

If you do not, as a person, leader in your life, personal life or anything, negating the process of thinking might spell doom. It is inevitable. I don't care how good or how successful you are right now. Eventually, everything that you've worked hard for might/will be lost because there's no act of thinking involved, because thinking allows us to catapult our lives and our careers to the next level. In the words of my surrogate mentor, Zig Ziglar, "Stinking Thinking," how to get rid of stinking thinking.

There are many individuals out there that says, well, motivational king, I understand that the lack of thinking   is not a good thing. So, one of the things that you must understand is that those are individuals that really think, and they think a lot. But what thoughts are they manifesting? Well, they're thinking negative thoughts, they're thinking thoughts of failure, thoughts of despair, of loss, and those thoughts will begin to manifest different things in their lives. They manifest the discord they may have on their business, manifests the discord they may have in their relationship, marriage, or what have you. So, you must understand that it doesn't matter.

Lack of thinking can cause problems, and a lack of certain thinking can cause bigger problems. So, if you have the condition called stinking thinking, the process by which you constantly and consistently think negative, it is bad and will tend to manifest in your life. As written in the book, "As a man thinketh so shall it be for him", whatever you think of, you're right. If you think you cannot succeed, then most likely you won't, and if you think you can, most likely you will.

Understand that for you to take your life, your career, your business to the next level; you must put yourself in a position of having the right thoughts of what you want to create. We are natural creators in life. We create things through our thoughts, minds, dreams etc. One thing that I understand is that dreams are free. You can dream for free, but actions require work for those dreams to come to fruition. We must have the right thought patterns in our minds to say how we're going to cultivate the idea and dreams we have.

I'm not saying merely having positive thoughts will get you there, because positive thoughts alone won't get you there. Positive thoughts reinforce through action, and a strong, unwavering belief, or should I say faith in what it is that you're trying to accomplish will allow you to accomplish that. Once you have that faith and you're thinking the right way, then you're equipped to take it to the next level, you have the right tools on you.

The right thinking or thoughts will turn up your thermostat, because you're only going to go as far as your thermostat is set to. It is not going to go beyond the limit you set for it through your thinking. If you aim higher by changing your thermostat through the way you think, you will be able to overcome and adapt to the different issues and struggles that you may face in your life. You must use your thinking cap and when you decide to think, it has to be positive, reaffirming faith full thoughts, and ideas.

It is one thing to have ideas and entirely a different thing to act on the ideas. Every idea unless worked upon will continue to remain dormant until an external force of thought acts on it to birth it into realities. Have you ever wondered what would have become of all the inventions we now have in the world if the people that caught a glimpse of the ideas decided to sleep over them and never allowed them to see the light of the day? I think your guess is as good as mine.

We have been created as humans with the ability to think; hence the name "Homo sapiens" if you cannot engage in proactive thinking as a human being then you have failed already. Now let's get this straight, thinking in the body of this context does not include worrying. When you begin to think about things you cannot change then you are worrying. I believe it will be totally insane for a man to think about how the sun will rise the next day or perhaps thinking of how to stop the sun from shining throughout the day. Think and worry less and you are on your way to becoming one of the most successful persons on earth. Only thinkers have the needed power to rule the world.

BRIDGE

Gina decided she would need a bath in order to help her recollect her thoughts and think of the best way to succeed in her new-found business idea. She was in high spirits when she left the sofa and walked to clear the table her kids had breakfast.

It took her about two hours to clear the dining table. After doing the dishes, Gina went to Amy's room, made the bed and then cleaned the room. After which, she went to Turner's room and had it cleaned.

By 10am, Gina walked to the small study located in the house and sat down. She took her notepad and stared hard at it. In the notepad, staring at her was her business plan.

"How would I get market?" She asked herself.

She knew there were many professional event planners in California and to make it, she had to make herself stand out. She had to choose whether to start a corporate event planning or a social event planning.

As she thought, Gina wrote down her points on her notepad. She weighed her options and decided to go into social event planning such as weddings, birthday, anniversaries and reunions.

As soon as she had established who her target market will be, Gina thought of the startup cost she would need for her business.

"I don't want to start small. I need to start big. Therefore, I will need to put in more money."

On her notepad, she wrote down the equipment she would need. She would need rent, equipment, inventory, communication, licenses and Taxes, payroll, advertising/ promotions, legal fees/accounting, miscellaneous, legal fees/ accounting as well as insurance. As she thought, she wrote them down on her pad and then the prices.

After high school, she had attended studied event planning. She had a degree in event planning. Immediately after graduation, Gina had decided to change career. She had gone back to school and had studied accounting.

"It is time I make use of my event planning university degree."

Finally, she decided that she would need a total of $28,000 to start up a social event planning business.

The next on her blueprint was how to operate her business.

"I will need an assistant, an event planning consultant, a part time bookkeeper as well as temporary employees would handle clerical work and help plan events."

She made a couple of phone calls and finally decided that

the following day, she would conduct her research.

She would also need to create an event design; she would also need to find a site. Gina realized she would have to make arrangement for food, decoration and entertainment.

She would also need to think of how to transport people to the event and from the event.

"I have to arrange for accommodations where necessary." She told herself.

She decided that she would also need to supervise the site to make sure that everything was working perfectly. Finally, Gina knew that to succeed, she would need to conduct evaluations of the events.

So deep in thought was Gina that she didn't know that it was getting late. She looked towards the clock and was surprised to realize that it was already 2pm.

"Goodness, I missed lunch."

She hurriedly dashed to the bathroom, had a bath and dressed in a pair of jeans and red shirt. The kids would be home in ten minutes.

By the time she made sandwich for herself and settled down to eat, she had almost thought of everything. She would have to clear her account and her savings. Gina wasn't bothered; she knew in a couple of years, she would get back her money.

Her eyes drifted to her late husband's picture on the wall. He had died three years ago in an auto crash on his way back home from work. Davis was the love of her life. She had never known she would survive losing him, but their kids had kept her going. Both Amy and Turner had Davis's ember eyes. She saw her husband in her kids.

Many a times, she had tried to date and fall in love, but Gina had never really found someone that filled her late husband's shoes. It had been three years and all she had was her job and her kids. They were her world.

The front door opened, and she heard the kids running into the house.

"Mom? We are home." Amy shouted. "I'm in the study." She called to them.

The kids walked into the study looking tired yet flushed.

They ran to her, engulfed her in a hug.

"So how was school today?" She asked them. "It was fun. We went to the cinema and..." Amy cut her brother off by waving at him. "That film is for kids."

"That's not what Miss Green said." Turner defended. "You are just seven. What do you know?"

Gina smiled at her kids and hugged them to her.

"Hey kids, do not squabble over trivial issues. Aren't you hungry?"

"I am not." Amy said and walked out.

"I want some sandwiches too." Turner told his mom.

"I will get you some."

He stared at the notepad on the table. "What are you writing mom?"

"That's my new business plan. I want to quit my job and go into event planning."

Turner frowned.

"Does that mean you would always be home when we get back from school?"

"Sweetheart I can't promise you that." "I love you mom."

"I love you too my darling." She said and ruffled his hair.

After about a minute of silent, she said,

"Now go upstairs, wash your hands and come back here for your sandwich."

He kissed her cheeks and walked out.

Gina took a last look at her notepad and beamed. She had thought of everything. All she needed to do now was to put her plans into actions.

4

CHAPTER 4

OPEN YOUR EYES, STOP FEEDING INTO THE LIES

Keep your ears open, your eyes open, grab everything you can, react, and learn!

-Victoria Abril

One thing I've noticed in life is this; majority of people consistently get most of their resources, facts, ideas, and base their opinions on what's on the television. Majority of people find it hard to differentiate between real and reel life. While real life is characterized with a lot of uncertainties, reel life is built based on a planned script which is acted in a controlled environment.

The television is something that tells its vision to you. You're simply getting your information from word of mouth, what friends and family talk about, or whatever propaganda that comes up. Basing our information, beliefs, habit, and whatsoever around these channels is simply building a mirage of sorts because we're building a foundation on falsified information. You cannot build your life based on the things you see on the screen. Your life will end in a total mess.

There are people who carry don't allow their research works to be influenced by what they find on the internet or the words of someone. They tend to carry out these research works outside their findings from sources or the resources at their disposal. These forms of research works may not be considered as credible.

Anyone can throw up a blog these days and say something or give their opinion. While there's nothing wrong with subjectivity, we need to have a certain sense of accurate and factual knowledgeable information coming from a reliable source.

There are different categories of people online. Most of them are hungry lions looking for the easiest way to earn a living and they tend to do this by spreading fake news or facts. They go online to post anything that comes to their mind and share it with the general public who have little or no idea of the dangers of wrong information. These innocent set of individuals tend to accept this fact because they found it online.

Since we are not aligning ourselves with the ability to feed our spirit our minds, our beliefs with positive, reaffirming, truthful and the right kind of information, our survival is hanging on a balance. Humans are now facing a greater threat of extinction from the world due to lack of information. Information is power and gaining access to it is as useful as the air we breathe. An individual who is not informed is heading for deformation.

So, we can't keep feeding into lies because when we're feeding ourselves lies, it's like waking up every day and eating a candy bar for breakfast, lunch, and dinner. Right now, that's not catastrophic. It won't hurt you right now. If you eat a candy bar for breakfast, lunch, and dinner for the next two weeks, most likely, you'll be okay. If you were to eat a candy bar for breakfast, lunch, and dinner for almost a month, you may begin to start having some problems.

But for the most part, immediately doing so won't be catastrophic, but let's just say you eat a candy bar for breakfast, lunch, and dinner for the next 10 years. I promise you it's going to be disastrous. It's simply a matter of time before all

those things are going to start compounding, like in the Dan Harding's book, "The Entrepreneur Rollercoaster."

Things tend to get compounded after going up. These things start compounding on you, and as it compounds, it's building little by little, little by little, little by little until it forms a mass that cannot be moved by any force whatsoever. And you're feeding yourself these questionable ideas. Hence, just because you believe something, does not mean it's real. You are entitled to your opinion which also has a greater chance of becoming false.

Les Brown, "someone's opinion of you does not have to be your reality," and there's so much more than what he's saying in that statement beyond the face value. Someone's opinion or your opinion of something doesn't necessarily need to correlate with reality. I may go out and say, well I don't believe in gravity, and then go from a six-story building and decide to jump. Whether or not you believe in gravity, doesn't mean it has anything to do with it reacting to you. Your belief has no power to change reality, it has no power to change established fact. The fact that you don't believe in ghosts doesn't mean they don't exist.

Understand your belief system, and what you stand boldly on. The platform that you stand and preach on may not be reality; it might not be something that can structurally stand the test of time. We must, always, base our beliefs and our systems and what we're going to do off true virtue, true belief and sound doctrine that will allow us to conduct our lives in a way that's going to be memorable, and that's how we'll be able to feed into our spirits and minds.

One noticeable thing in life is most people are walking zombies. They may appear living outside but deep down inside they are not better than dead bodies lying in the morgue waiting to be buried. They are not better than remote controlled puppets which are waiting for the next command from their wrong beliefs and fear to spring into action. I said this because it's the bitter unpalatable truth. The truth is bitter even when delivered in sugar coated speeches. Whether or not we want to admit to it, at the end of the day, most people are walking zombies. They don't pay attention. They're creatures of habit, not creatures of creation. The life they now live is totally an opposite of what they were created to be.

They lack a sense of direction and cannot go through life without listening to their fears and wrong habits. There is a need for us to understand that we've been placed here to be creatures of creation, and not habit. You are here for a reason and that very reason is not found in your habit. You know how I wake up in the morning and have a cup of coffee and smoke a cigarette, that's a habit. What are we creating? What are we trying to leave behind for the future generation? Will they be glad we lived or will curse us for turning the world upside down? Think deeply about these things.

Humans from inception are creators and it is our duty to make sure we practice the act of creation daily. Here is a question I will love you to ask yourself daily. What am I creating today? Have I been able to stay true to my cause today? What did I create in today's 24 hours?

What are we creating in our lives? What are we creating in other people's lives? We need to live a life of sharing all what we have with others. But we're so easy to get into the propaganda of life that we never open our eyes.

We just follow, we don't feel and touch the person in front of us, we just follow their lead. We don't even open our eyes. We just feed into whatever's being told to us. Whatever makes us feel comfortable. If you're willing to do what is hard today, then your life will ultimately be easy. It's so easy to do the wrong thing and it's so hard to do the right thing. And most people will never understand the importance of opening one's eyes and being your own individual. Understand that everyone else is taken, so be yourself.

I challenge you to be the best person that you can be. I challenge you to challenge yourself, not to try to compete with the other person, not feeding into the lies that they're telling about how they feel about their life when, in truth, they don't feel this way. Just because it looks good on the surface that they're doing okay, and life is so good for them doesn't mean they're not going through utter hell. But if you try to compare yourself to them, and you try to compete with somebody else that's not even in your lane, then you are missing the point. You are the best version of yourself, you are unique in your own way that is why your appearance is quite different than every other person on earth. There is no need to live a life trying to please others, there is no need to live a life trying to look like others. You are the best the world has ever seen and will ever witness. You are a gift to the world.

Create your own destiny yourself. Think for yourself. Stop feeding into lies of what other people are telling you regarding who you should be. People will always want you to be like them, they will never cease to judge you by their weaknesses. Listening to their lies will only limit you to their power, it will drag you down to their level and leave you to dwell there as a lost sheep. Let them tell themselves what they should be, and you start telling yourself what you should be. It is your time, you are the one. You are the creator. You are the one to create your life and your destiny.

You may take the interpretation of what your friends or family is saying. But ultimately, you should think for yourself. Understand the importance of thinking. Understand that you must open your eyes and use your visual cortex to be able to look out into the horizon and see what is before you.

Glance at what's behind you to see where you're at in order to take it to the next level, just because someone said something to you does not mean it has to be your reality. And once you get to that level, once you become that person, you ultimately will see yourself in a whole new level. It is not possible for the other person because he approached the whole situation with his personality, try solving the problem using a different approach and you will surely get your answer. Life is a mathematical equation with several X and Y's your ability to apply the right formulas will determine how you arrive at your answer. Be positive, you are a gift to the whole world.

BRIDGE

Later that evening, she was taking a nap when her cellphone rung.

"Hello?" Gina said in a husky tone.

"Sweetheart..." She heard her friend's soprano's tone. "Hello Angela. How is your honeymoon going?"

Angela had married the love of her life two weeks ago. She was Gina's best friend and the only person Gina had told about challenges she was facing at work.

"Guess what?" Angela asked.

"You're pregnant." Gina supplied with a beam. "Sweetheart, I got married two weeks ago. I don't even

know if am pregnant or not-yet."

"Then what's it?" Gina asked her friend.

"Ken and I decided to cut short our honeymoon and return home." She was laughing at the other side of the line.

"You mean you're in California?"

"Sure girl. I'm back. I missed you and I also missed the kids."

"We missed you too love."

"How about Ken and I come over for dinner?" "Oh, that would be great."

"We shall get a bottle of wine on our way over." Angela supplied.

"Oh, that would be great. I look forward to seeing your ever-radiant face again."

They both laughed.

"Mom, I need your help with a sum." Amy said, appearing at the doorway.

"I've got to go Angel. See you by 7pm?" "Sure sweet. Bye."

Gina pressed the end button. She turned to her daughter.

"That's Angela; she's back from her honeymoon with Ken."

Amy's eyes glittered. "Did she get me some candy?"

Gina kissed her daughter's cheeks. "Darling, she went on her honeymoon not shopping."

She helped her daughter with her homework. When they were through, it was already 4pm. Gina decided to surf the net for more insight on how to run her new event planning business.

She typed on the word event planning and stared in horror at the write-ups before her. Blogs after blogs, she read.

A blog said that event planners in California were too many. The competition was so high that venturing into it would be a waste of time. Gina was surprised. She left the page and clicked on another.

After about thirty minutes, Gina was discouraged. The blogs she had read had more of negative things to say about event planning than positive things. Gina was disappointed.

By 5pm, she slowly walked to the kitchen to start preparing dinner. She decided to prepare oven baked peach cobblers topped with Blue Bell Vanilla ice cream.

As she made dinner, Gina thought of the best way to not get discouraged. What she had read online was not encouraging at all. After cooking, Gina dashed upstairs for a shower. It was summer and the heat was too much.

After bathing, she dressed in another pair of blue jeans and a sleeveless red top. By 7pm, the doorbell rang, and she went to get it. With a single yank, Gina pushed open the door. Angela stood there in a short evening dress and a pair of red court shoes. Her long charcoal black hair was made into a ponytail. She looked younger, alive and satisfied.

"Oh Angela!" Gina exclaimed.

The two women embraced each other. After what seemed like ages, Gina stepped back and looked at her friend's radiant face again.

"Marriage seems to treat you well." Gina observed. "Ken is treating me well."

"I have to, you're now my responsibility." A deep male voice said behind her.

Gina looked up and her eyes locked with Ken's brown eyes. He was tall, dark and slim. He sent her a smile and Gina couldn't help but smile back. He opened his arms and Gina walked into them. She loved his cologne.

"You look great." Ken whispered in her ears. "Thank you."

The three friends walked into the house. Angela helped Gina set the table. The kids came down and they all had a quiet dinner.

"How is your work going?" Angela asked Gina.

Gina knew that her friend was asking her if she had resolved the problem she was having in her working place.

"Mom hardly went to work anymore." Turner supplied.

"Don't be a child. Mom is on her annual leave." Amy smirked at her brother.

"I am not a child." He said getting angry.

"Come on kids, eat your food and stop squabbling." Angela told the kids with a beautiful smile on her face.

The children continued eating.

"Well, the issue had been resolved." Gina said carefully.

"Oh, that's great. When will you be returning to work?" She asked her friend.

"Actually Angela, I've decided I don't want to return to the IT firm. It is high time I double my worth and think about making a better investment for myself."

Angela took a sip of her wine. She looked up at her friend and smiled.

"If you don't go back to work, what would you do?"

"I intend starting my own event planning business. I have a degree in event planning."

"Really? Wow, I never knew." Ken asked looking very surprised.

"After college, my I had my first degree in event planning. After I had my degree, I lost interest in it and decided to be an accountant instead."

"That's good." Ken said, smiling reassuring at her.

"Why ever would you say that? Gina here had never been into this business. There are a lot of event planners. Do you think she would survive?" Angela asked with a frown.

"Of course, she shall survive." Ken said.

Angela waved her hands at him. Turning to Gina she said, "Don't even do it. It is time consuming. Who would take care of the kids in the evenings? Besides, I heard it isn't a lucrative venture."

Gina felt her anger rising but she said nothing. She knew all that she had read in the internet and all that her friend was telling her were lies. She knew she would succeed.

"Don't do it Gina." Angela begged.

Gina flashed Angela her best smile.

"I have decided Angel, there is no turning back now. Can you please wish me luck?"

Angela shifted uncomfortably in her chair. "Well, good luck."

Gina smiled. Humans ventured into the business of event planning and they survived. They were not better than her. She decided to not listen to lies again and go into action. It was time she moved on. It was time she doubled her worth.

5

CHAPTER FIVE

STOP RELAXING WHEN YOU SHOULD BE TAKING ACTION

Take time to deliberate; but when the time for action arrives, stop thinking and go in.

-Andrew Jackson

One of the friendliest enemies' man has ever had is rest. Most people just want to relax. They want to kick back with their feet up when they ought to understand that the life we live is not a dress rehearsal. We're are live on stage and all we do counts. In life we will not be fortunate enough to retrace our steps or restart all over again when we miss a line. This is the show. You just showed up. You came here to give people what they want to see. It should reflect oneself and ultimately, where they should aim to be. That's what you should tell yourself, and that's how others should look at you. But why are we relaxing when we should be in action? The war has just begun. Why are we eating sandwiches? Understand that there's going to come a time when you're going to have to take a rest and take a breath, but those breaths must be short. That rest must be short.

Why are we relaxing? Why does everything have to be such a microwave society where we put it on for a couple of seconds and then we can eat, and we can enjoy our life? But what is your competition doing? Is your competition operating that way? I guarantee that they're not. They're going out there and they're making things happen, they are innovators. And then, most people will say, "well, I don't believe what you're saying right now in this text," and that's okay since everyone is entitled to his or her opinions.

Understand this: while you doubt what I'm saying, go and look at your bank account statements. Go look at the pile of bills that's on your desk right now, if you even have a desk. If you're in your one-bedroom studio apartment with less than two or three hundred square feet, and realize that what I'm saying is true, that you must invest -- it must be a sum of your conclusion. It must be a product of your conclusion, what you want for yourself.

You can doubt, and you may choose not to believe what I'm saying, and that's okay. But understand that what I'm telling you is a way for you to change your life. I'm giving you the unadulterated truth about my perspective on life. Whether or not that's right or wrong; that's someone's objective opinion about my works and what I do. What I'm telling you is based on my experience, is that you don't have time to be resting right now. Look at your life. Evaluate what's around you right now and ask yourself honestly, is it time for me to kick back and relax or is it time for me to get in gear and start working toward the things that I want in this life?

You have no right to go to sleep without making enough money to settle the next day's bill. Life is so unfair because the moment you wake up to face it, the meter is already counting.

It's time for you to start thinking and start believing and start dreaming again. That's what time it is in your life. It's not a time to relax. It's time for you to act, and when I say, "take action," I mean a systematic way of thinking, of

formulating a strategy to be able to put into action, to catapult your life to the next level, and that's what this thing's about. It's not about just sitting around evaluating and talking. A lot of people give any situation a good lip service, but I want you to get out of the habit of giving lip service.

Stop giving a situation lip service and start giving it action. Act today. Don't wait to act until you've finished completing the book. Act today while you're reading the text. So, you know what? From this point on, I'm going to change my life. I'm going to take my life in a whole new direction. I'm ready. I challenge you to do that. I challenge you to think in a whole new way. Think about your life. Think about your family, your legacy. I challenge you. Think about the things that really count and not the things you can count on. The things that really count may not be counted, but they surely are worth the pain and sacrifice.

I dare you to act right now. I challenge you to take control. I challenge you to stop relaxing and take control of your life. I challenge you to go to work. I challenge you to act. I know there's someone out there, because I have challenged you. You're going to take me up on it, but I challenge you for the next 90 days, to go out. Don't quit like you've done before. Don't say, well I'm going to start running today and by the end of the week you're not running anymore. I challenge you to say that you're strong enough under any condition. I challenge you to challenge all your challenges, I dare you to dare all the darts pointing at you. I challenge you to be a better person.

I challenge you to take your life in a whole other direction. Because it takes that type of person and the fact that how you do something, is how you do everything. Don't wait and say that you're going to change your life, that you'll wait until you finish this book; you're going to wait till you've read the next book, you must wait to see the video. No, you don't have to wait for any of those things. I want you to go out, right now. The best time to act is now or never. Every dream comes with an expiry date written on them. If you fail to meet the deadline, the dream becomes something you once had, leaving you to bite the finger of regret.

It's time to stop relaxing because your competition is not relaxing, they're out there making things happen. That's why they got the car that they wanted, the house that they desired. That's why they go on the vacations you wish you could go on. They have the things that you wish that you could have, that you only can dream about because you don't have the passion or the conviction in you right now to go after it yourself. It's up to you to take yourself to the next level, the things that you want, you're going to have to do some things you've never done. You cannot do the same thing and expect a different result; only mad men do that. If you want better results, be better.

You must become something you've never been in order to have the things that you've never had. But for some people, that doesn't move them. They live in what we call "someday I'm going to make it happen" world. Someday I'm going to get off my butt and do something big. Someday is

a not a day. What about today. What about Monday, what about Wednesday, what about Friday? I'm going to start today. And that's my question to you, I challenge you, when are you going to start? When will you dissociate from that friendly enemy called rest and get to work?

When are you going to start living a life that you're supposed to live? When are you going to start chilling, when are you going to stop telling yourself, well if I had just given it just a little bit more, I would have done it? You're scared of success, that's why you keep self-sabotaging yourself. Every time you start that new business, you wind up not paying your fees to stay in business. You wind up not paying your dues to stay in business. You wind up pissing somebody else off, so you can't stay in business, because, deep inside, you believe if you go out that way, you won't look like a failure because if you give it your all and you tell everybody you gave it your all and you fail, then you look like a failure.

But ladies and gentlemen, understand this, failure is a situation and not an individual, it's not a person. Stop self- sabotaging yourself, turn the thermostat just a little bit higher. I challenge you to go a little bit further. Give yourself 90 days to unload on everything. Put your head down and go for it like you've never gone for it before. Stop being a chicken and equip yourself with the tools that you need to go ahead. Stop letting the competition beat you. It is time to set the pace. You can beat the competition and set a record for others to beat. Usain Bolt is one of the fastest men the world has ever seen, he always goes to the track with one

determination; to beat his previous record. You can also do the same. Remember that it is not over until you believe it is over. You can do something now. You can start acting now. The clock is ticking away, and your dreams will soon become a thing of the past. Have you ever wondered what would have happened if Bill Gates had rested a bit before starting up Microsoft; his dream would have expired; he would have had an invalid dream.

BRIDGE

A week later, Gina was in the laundry room doing her laundry while thinking of the new business she was about to start. A lot of things needed to be done. For instance, she would need to open a domain name, she would need to get an office and pay the rent. She would also need to go out and shop for the equipment she would need for her business.

"I have so much to do." She thought out loud. All she wanted now was to get started. Her boss, Jack had paid her a visit the previous day. She had been surprised to see him standing in front of her door.

In the six years she had worked for the firm, he had visited only once- when her husband had died. She heard the doorbell rang and had ran downstairs to get it. She was dressed in short yellow sleeveless dress.

"Hi Georgina." He had said.

Jack was dressed in a pair of brown chinos trousers, dark green T shirt and a pair of boat shoes. Although he was

in his mid-forties, he had managed to maintain his body by spending two hours daily at the gym. He had broad chest and a strong muscular body.

"May I come in?" He had asked when she made no effort to invite him in.

"Of course, Jack, please do come in."

He walked into the room and sat on the sofa. "What can I offer you? Bear, wine?"

"Water would do." He said.

It was still morning and her kids had gone to school. Gina had ran to the fridge and brought him a glass of water. Jack took a sip and then turned to her.

"Please sit-down Georgina."

Gina took a seat and turned to look at him. She knew what this was all about. She had received countless emails and phone calls from the firm to return to work, but she had not made any effort to.

"I know you are angry with me Gina, but as an accountant, you should have known it was only fair we investigate all that had happened under your watch."

Gina almost laughed at her boss, but she smiled.

"Jack, I am not angry with you. I understand that you did the right thing. I should have known that Carl was carting away money from the firm."

"You should have but you trusted him too much and he betrayed that trust. Your name has been cleared but you still haven't returned to work. It's been a week already. The firm needs an accountant."

Gina knew she would never return to her former place of work. No, she wanted something different.

"So, what do you say about returning to work tomorrow?" He asked looking directly into her eyes.

"I will be at the firm tomorrow." She supplied. She could

see him smiling excitedly.

"Jack, I shall come to formerly tender my resignation." The smile immediately disappeared from his face. "What did you just say?"

"I am quitting Jack. After staying at home for a whole month, I have lost interest in the cooperate world. I want to venture into something else."

"What is that?"

"I have decided to venture into event planning and decor." "Georgina, if you come back, I shall increase your salary

by 50%."

By now Georgina had known her worth. She had blatantly refused the man's offer.

"Think about it Gina."

"There is nothing to think about."

Gina smiled to herself as she recalled the conversation between her former boss and herself. She had already resigned but she was yet to start her business.

She had not even created time to go for market survey.

"Why are you resting Gina? You need to sit up and start acting." She chided herself.

When she was through with her laundry, Georgina walked to her fridge and retrieved a can of coke.

It had been a week she had decided to start her own event planning business, yet she had relaxed so much that she had done nothing. She hasn't been out to hunt for an office, she didn't have a site yet and she was yet to get the equipment she would need.

Procrastination is dangerous. She thought to herself.

"If I continue to relax and procrastinate, I will not be able to achieve my dreams. I have submitted my resignation. Why am I dallying?"

As she took a gulp at the coke in her hands, Gina decided, it was time she began acting. Faith without works is useless. She must wake up and start working.

With that in mind, she dashed upstairs, change into

another dress wore a pair of black stiletto heels and picked up her car keys.

If she continued like this, she would use the capital she has for her business into doing something else. She had to act very quickly. She had decided to double her worth by not working for anyone. She would prove to her friend, Angela that despite what she thought, she would make it big in the event planning world.

As she stepped out of her house, the afternoon breeze blew her hair. She was going office hunting. She was determined to start her business in less than a month come what. There was no time to dally any more.

"I am about to become popular." She told herself as she unlocked her Blue Toyota Camry and boarded the car.

She knew that she would be successful, and she would soon give her kids a very comfortable life.

"Procrastination is indeed dangerous. I will not delay a day longer."

6

CHAPTER SIX

GET EQUIPPED OR GET WHIPPED

Some people dream of success, while other people get up every morning and make it happen.

-Wayne Huizenga

T hat does it really mean to Get equipped or get whipped? Most people go through life and ill equipped. They take each day as it is and are satisfied with whatsoever outcome they obtain. The worst fight that you can ever get into is a fight where you have all the necessary tools to compete, but you don't understand how to use the tools you have. Understanding is one vital tool that men tend to neglect in their day to day activity. This understanding comes from the acquisition of knowledge.

The scenario that will be used is that of The Indiana Jones movie when Indiana Jones was looking for his escape; and this real good swordsman blocks the way. So, when the swordsman starts swinging the sword back and forth and displaying all these elaborate tricks, Indiana Jones simply looks in amusement and after the swordsman bigger than life show is over Indiana Jones pulls his gun out and shoots him dead and carries on with his business. As funny as that may seem, that's how most people get killed in life when it comes to their dreams, because their competition is pulling out the gun and shooting them every time, while they're coming up with this elaborate sword. That sword is supposed to make them look good, it's supposed to make them feel good, make them feel that they're doing something.

They look the part. But when it comes to time to putting in the action and the work that's required, they fall short. Every now and then they flash their swords before their competitors hoping to instill fear in them. While they are busy thinking of a way to make their competition afraid, the competition is busy devising means to take them out of the equation. At the end of the day, they find themselves at the mercy of failure because they have succeeded in giving their competition the upper hand of success.

They're swinging the sword and looking clean- cut, but they can never deliver the blow to make it to the next level. They can never deliver that killer crushing move needed to make a move onto the next level, because the only thing they showed up to do is just put on all appearances. They want to look good, just for looks. In life, it's not about just for looks, you got to be able to be a person of action, so if you're not properly equipped with the tools, or if you don't know your limitations, okay, so who's more powerful, the person that just doesn't know their limitations, or the person that knows their limitations and what they need to do, but they make slight adjustments so they know exactly what they're limited to, or the person just doesn't know their ignorance of their own capabilities.

These are people that normally don't make it far in life because they are ignorant. They don't know what they don't know, but a person that knows, hey, I don't have the education, I don't have the expertise, I don't come from a family that's well-tutored, I don't have a family of high influence, and I know this. I'm going into the game knowing these things. How can I compensate for that? Well, how do I equip myself with the right tools to be able to compensate for my shortcomings? What these exceptional people have been known to do, even though they may not come from aristocratic families, what they've been able to do, have an unwavering work ethic. So, what they do is that they equip themselves with a work ethic that's unparalleled to anyone else, therefore compensating all the things that they lack.

See, what losers and people that are less confident in themselves continue to do is to place their shortcomings in front, because in their minds, they believe that well, I'm never good enough. So, I'm never good enough equates to I never can get what I want. But what they don't understand is that, no matter where you come from, what attributes you have or don't have, if you're properly equipped, you can overcome any situation and have anything you want to have, but you have to position yourself in a position that you're able to equip yourself under any circumstance. You must accept the fact that you need help to understand how everything works, you have to admit that you need assistance to achieve some certain goals. You can never get to your destination alone, you need people to guide you through, you need to hear people's stories and tap from their pool of knowledge.

One thing that we must understand when we say you must get equipped is that being equipped means you have the tools for success. Having the tools and being properly prepared for any situation that may come your way allows you to capitalize on the situation. Anything short of that is not going to allow you success, and that is where most people fail. This is where everything stops, and this is what separates the winners from the losers. Most people that have never experienced success in their life, will tell you that those individuals that are successful have only done so because they are lucky.

They're overwhelmingly lucky. They came from a good family. They came from good fortune. But what a winner knows for a fact is, no matter what the situation is, there is always a chance of losing. It does not matter what your background is. It does not matter how much money you have, how much education you have. The bitter truth about life is this; Luck does not exist, it is a fairy tale, it does not work for anybody. People who have been able to succeed in life were not just lucky, they also had to pay the price to be well equipped for opportunity when it came knocking at the door. They were sensitive enough to allow themselves pass through series of trainings just to be ready for the forthcoming opportunity that they never even believe would come their way someday.

At the end of the day, the drawing board is always an even playing ground. It is how you set up the play, how you are properly equipped to play the game, that allows you to capitalize or not. Now, with, for those people, so you've got to realize, one of my mentors always says this, he said, "there are three types of people in this world. The first person is called a winner. The second person is a loser. And then there are people that have not figured out how to win yet.

There are people out there who feel as if they are winners, but they've never experienced a victory. They've never had a breakthrough. It's not because something's wrong with them. It's not because they didn't have the right opportunity. It's because they lack preparation, because they have not equipped themselves with the proper tools or they fail to understand what tools that they need to put in their box. They have a large empty tool box which is crying to be filled with the right tools daily, they have a workshop which has been lying in ruins because they cannot bring themselves to really master the art of identifying the right tools and how to use them.

They fail to understand what tools are needed to put on their belt to complete the job at hand. And when you fail to know what tools you need or you fail to understand how those tools are what you need in order to take your life, and business, to the next level, then you are always going to repeat the same things again. You're always going to be on the same level, the same board, and always must continuously repeat the same challenges, and never figure out why you don't have success. So, what you've got to understand, is at the end of the day, either you get equipped, or you're going to get whipped every single time.

It does not matter what your ethnicity is. It doesn't matter what your background is, it doesn't matter how much money you have in the bank. Some of the best and brightest people have made fortunes overnight, and they've lost fortunes overnight. We all have the same time, the same capabilities. It does not matter. It's what you're putting in your tool belt, it's what you're putting in your toolbox that's going to allow you to perpetuate your life forward in an upward progression. You can never win a battle with the wrong weapon. Weapons come in different categories with distinct purposes. The fact

that a razor blade is sharp doesn't mean you can use it to cut down a tree, the fact that an axe is sharp, doesn't mean you can use it to cut your nails. Choose the right weapon and your work will be easier.

Anything short of not knowing or properly equipping yourself and you're going to end up like the swordsman in the Indiana Jones movie. While you're up playing games and trying to look good, your competition is working on being good and being great and being the best. So, I challenge you to be your best, be better than just good, know exactly what you want, and go for it and properly equip yourself with all the tools necessary to make your life a success. Carry out the necessary search and know all the tools you require to achieve success in life. you can be better with the right tools. Wake up and get to work.

BRIDGE

Another week later, Gina was in the study, making budgets and plans. After three days of searching, she had gotten a nice shop in Beverly Hills. The previous occupant had moved to Los Angeles a few weeks back. She had paid the rent with her credit card. After paying the rent, she had taken Amy and Turner to see it.

"Oh mom, it's beautiful." Amy exclaimed. The shop was located close to a diner.

"Does that mean you would be working late?" Her son asked her.

Gina sighed.

"I will be working late because most events take place in the evenings."

"Who would take care of us?" Turner asked.

"I don't need a baby sitter. I am a big girl." Amy shouted at her brother.

"Don't be mean to your brother Amy. Don't forget he is the only sibling you have, and he is younger than you." Gina chided.

Amy looked down at her shoes guiltily.

"Now my darlings, you're right. I will be working late. But I want you to know that I love you more than anything. I love you more than this business itself, but I have to work in order to put food in your stomach, pay your school fees, provide a roof for you to sleep at night and get clothes for you."

The kids listened attentively to her.

"We all have to make sacrifices kids. I may be busy in the evenings, but I shall get a live-in housekeeper to help take care of you."

"I don't want a housekeeper," Amy said with tears in her eyes.

"Don't say that sweet. I am your mother. No house keeper will ever take my place in your heart."

Amy ran to her mother and engulfed her in a hug.

"I love you mom."

"I love you to my sweethearts. Never forget that mommy loves you."

In order to get properly equipped for what lay ahead, Gina needed to get legal licenses. She got her general business license approved. She had decided to sell event planning items such as food, equipment settings and utensils. She was smart enough to also get a seller permit. Getting a resale license wasn't also difficult to get.

Gina also managed to get a federal tax Identity number and a state employment number because she would have to hire caterers, an assistant, an accountant and a consultant. Once that was achieved, she knew she had gotten herself halfway equipped to start working.

Gina created a website and a domain name. She decided to name her business "Exquisite event planning."

The domain was now under construction. Of course, it would cost her almost a fortune, but she knew it was worth it.

"I need insurance."

She registered her business for insurance. That also would cost a fortune, but it didn't matter.

"Mom?" Her son asked her the following day. "Yes?"

"What events are you planning?"

Gina smiled at him.

"I will be hosting birthdays, celebrations, anniversaries, parties and even dinners."

"Will you be paid?" "Of course."

"Can I help you?"

"Yes, you can help me Turner by attending school and taking your school work very serious."

"Okay mom."

Gina had been so busy that she only got to see her kids in the evenings. She returned, tired and hungry. Now she would need to hire a consultant, an accountant, and an assistant. She advertised the job position online.

Before the end of another week, she had gotten ten applications in different areas. She decided to interview the applicants online, using Skype. It was successful.

She now had an assistant, a consultant and an accountant.

She had also decided she would need to go shopping. "I am on my way to be an event planner."

It hurt her to realize she would be too busy in the evenings for her kids but to succeed, one needed to make sacrifices. She could never sacrifice her kids, no. She could always create time to know them better.

"Are you sure this is what you want?" Angela asked her over the phone that evening.

"Of course, Angel. I am suddenly tired of the cooperate world."

"For crying out Gina you are an accountant."

"I am also an event planner. By the way, don't forget I was an event planner before I became an accountant."

Her friend sighed from the other side of the line. "I am worried about you."

"Why are you worried Angie? I am a fully-grown woman.

I am an adult."

"I know that love. I also know that you love being an accountant."

"I loved being in accountant. It's all in the past."

Angela laughed and Gina relished at the sound of her friend's voice.

"Tell me. Are you fully equipped?"

"I am almost through. I now have business license, I have a federal Identity number and a state employment letter."

"That is great. So, are you going to be hiring helpers?"

"Sure, I will. I guess I must have forgotten to mention that I now have employed an assistant, an accountant and a consultant."

"Jeez girl, do you really need an accountant? You are an accountant."

"I had to hire one. I realized that my schedule is about to become tedious and I don't want to add to it."

"Oh, that's understandable."

"Oh yes, I have also decided to name my business "The exquisite.""

Angela smiled.

"I love that. Don't worry girlfriend, I can see that you're truly well equipped. Don't worry, we got your back. I shall put in words about you to my husband's business associates and my colleagues."

"I would really appreciate that love. Thanks a million." "This is the little support I can offer you."

"You did well. Thank you." "So how are the kids taking it?"

"Well, they don't like the idea of a live-in housekeeper but I'm sure they will get used to it. They are smart and intelligent."

"Yes. Their father was also smart and intelligent. Don't you think it's high time you started dating again?"

"Can you please send my love to Ken? I need to make an important call."

Angela laughed. She knew her friend was deliberately avoiding that topic. The line went dead in seconds and Gina realized that she was now well equipped. She had almost everything ready.

7

CHAPTER SEVEN

IN ORDER TO WIN YOU MUST CHANGE WITHIN

I had to get beat to understand how to win.

-Bob Beamon

So many people will say, well I don't need much; the simple things matter. I would argue that, for the most part, there's nothing wrong with that. Everyone has and values things differently. But for some people, life is beating them up so bad, they feel as if their greatness has been stripped from them. So, before that, they would tell the world what it is they want to do in a big fashion and in a big form, they would just cover it or camouflage it with subtleties of, I just want to be simple; I just want to be plain. I don't want to put myself out there just to get hurt. I really value my sanity and I cannot put it on the line to be different. I am satisfied with what I have, and I don't think I need to be better in anyway. I don't really place values on some of those things, just let me stay on this lane for now, I am well satisfied with everything.

I had a real good job and I lost it. I had a real good career then I knew I was going to retire, and he let me go. My kids are getting older, I've had to switch five, six different schools. My kids don't look at me the same way. I feel as if I'm losing more than I'm gaining. So right now, it doesn't take much to make me happy, but you're ultimately conditioning yourself mentally to believe something that your heart is not in love with. Your heart is not in love with the fact that you're willing to settle for something lesser than you're capable of doing just because it fits the current situation right now.

The present situation is that we just need a little bit   to survive. We need just a little bit to make it to the next level. The reason you've got to give it your all is because, just imagine that you're in a football game and you're on the field and giving it all that you have, at the end of the game,

even if you lose, it doesn't hurt as much because you knew you gave it your all, and you left it all on the field. The best feeling in life doesn't always come from winning but from knowing that you gave in your best while trying to win. Life is not all about winning, the greatest people on earth are not actually winners but losers who learned the art of winning while giving it their best.

But when your half-butt it, when your half-ass it, when you go through and you know that you didn't give it your all, and then you lose, that really hurts, because you know you could have done better. But when you give it your all, it just puts it in a different category. Well, you can accept the loss better and look at your situation and say to yourself, "well, I gave it my all and still didn't win. Maybe I need to learn something else to make me stronger so I'm able to win next time. Because if I knew I had everything, if I was properly equipped with what I needed, guess what, I know I would have won. I knew I gave it my all. I knew I tried my best, I knew I gave in all I had but it was just not enough, perhaps I should try harder next time.

That's all I had to give. So, if I don't have any more to give, there's no way I could have won. But if I had more, maybe I need to give myself more, so that next time, when I go up against them, I am able to win. One problem with most people is that they're not willing to change within or how they look and value things. Their perception in life and what they'll do is they'd rather settle instead of changing who they are. They'd rather force other people to change or change

their perspective of how they look at you. See, the problem with that is most people are not going to change. The only person that can change is you and if you don't change, then how in the world are you ever going to change your situation. The power to change your situation lies strictly in your hands. If your situation must change, then you must complement the action by changing your perceptions, beliefs and attitude towards life. There is no way we can expect other people to change when we cannot effect change in ourselves. If we want our situations to change, then we must change ourselves. When we can change ourselves, we are changing from within, and that's how we win. The greatest battle is the one fought in the mind. If you can win the battle in your mind, you will surely win over every situation in your life.

You cannot win if you don't master yourself. You must be in a position of vulnerability with yourself, to have an unconditional understanding and truthfulness with yourself. Because one thing we all know is that we can fool other people, but we cannot fool ourselves. We can fool ourselves mentally to believe something or adopt a concept mentally, people do it every day. They trick themselves to believe that they like their job that they have based on the premise that that's the best job they can have. But if they had their own options, they would be doing something else that they truly love. What they're doing right now pays the bills and that's okay, so at least if I'm going to do it, let me try to fall in love with it.

Well, we're not in love with it, we're in love with the idea of what it can do for our current situation and our heart is in no way, form, or shape in love with doing something that it is not in tune with. If you want to find your passion, your true belonging in life, be guided by your heart. Now, there are a lot of different phraseologies out here about the love in your heart and how the heart can deceive you, but ultimately, I think that's all subjective.

I think the one thing that can be deceived is the mind. I honestly believe that the soul is a direct line to the heart, and the heart for some reason almost has a tendency that we get that feeling in our heart, we get that feeling in our gut or what have you. It is coming when something just isn't right or doesn't quite sit with us. But what we do is we poison our heart by telling ourselves that the feeling that we have is not real, that what we think is truly the truth and what we ultimately believe in, even though our heart tells us the opposite. So, who's really trying to fool who? Is it the mind lying to the heart, or is the heart lying to the mind?

In my opinion, it's the mind lying to the heart, trying to convince the heart that it's okay to be less than what we're capable of doing, which in my perception and my mind is ludicrous. It does not make any sense. In order to change, you've got to change. If nothing changes, nothing changes. If you want to win, you must change within. What's inside of you, what are you putting inside of you? What have you been telling yourself? How are you looking at things, your perception of things because all of self?

What are you reading? Who are you associating yourself with? Who are you aligning yourself with? What audience are you entertaining? Those things are ultimately going to dictate where your life is headed. Not your past, but your present, because now your present will soon be your past, and what is your future will soon be your present. Think cautiously, think fearfully, move forward and remember, in order to win you must change from within. The change starts from what you are looking at, because you can never be better than your role model, the change stats from what you feed your mind with. The more junk you allow your mind to have access to daily, the more complicated your life gets. The change starts from changing your company, because you can never be better than who you associate with. If you are really interested in changing your life, you need to change your company, you need to be careful with what you allow your heart gain access to daily, you need to watch your ways and guard your heart with all diligence because it is the wellspring of life.

The power to change comes from within and not without. What you believe in will surely have a way of changing your perception about things. If you believe you can make it, then you surely can, but when you allow your mind to settle for less than your best, you will surely end up living a defeated life with little or no result to show for it. You can be better than your yesterday; you can make today count so that tomorrow will be great. You can rewrite the future. You have the power to make a change and become what you want to be. If you can see it, you can achieve it.

BRIDGE

Three weeks had come and left since Gina had decided to change her career in accounting and start event planning and decor. She had carefully chosen to take on social event planning and she was really looking excited with her achievement.

At first, she had toyed with the idea of starting her own business. She had relaxed and had chided herself by waking up from her slumber and getting back on her feet. For the past two weeks, Gina had been up and doing, determined to let no one discourage her or her effort. The fact that others tried event planning and failed didn't meant that she would also fail.

To succeed, you need to change.

She had read it online and Gina was on her way to change. She was determined to change for the better. She was determined to cut some people out of her life.

Fred, her late husband's brother always insisted on taking her out on dinner dates. A month ago, he had tried to seduce her.

So deep in thought was Gina she didn't hear her phone beeped.

"Mom, your phone is beeping." Amy told her.

"Thanks, my love." Gina retorted and picked the phone.

Fred's name appeared on the screen.

"Talk about the devil." She murmured and pressed the receive button.

"Hi Gina."

"Hi Fred." She retorted.

"Good evening. How are you and the kids?" "We are all doing great. How is your wife?" "She is fine. How is your work?"

Gina held the phone tightly in her hands. "Actually Fred, I quit my job two weeks ago." "What? Are you crazy?"

"What do you mean?" She asked him.

"I mean, that job pays you well enough. What else do you need?"

"I don't owe you an explanation Fred, do I?"

"Of course, you do. I am Davis's brother and he left you in my care."

"Oh really?" She placed her hands on her hips.

Gina left the sofa and climbed the stairs to her room. She

didn't want Amy to witness her fight with Fred.

"Of course. He left you that house but don't forget that the house needs maintenances."

She opened her bedroom door and stepped into the room. When she shut the door behind her, Gina climbed into bed.

"Now you listen to me Fred, I am sick and tired of you meddling in my affairs. Back off."

"I am the only father the kids know."

"You can never be their father. Your first mistake was trying to seduce me during our last dinner. I forgave you but I will never forget."

Gina had never spoken to him in that manner before.

Fred was surprised.

"What has come over you?"

"I am now a changed person Fred. I am not the quiet woman you met twenty years ago."

"Well, I'm sure you're fucking someone already. I've always known you're a slut."

Gina clutched the phone closer to her ears. She was so angry that she was shaking like a leaf.

"You are no longer welcome to my house." "That's not your house. My brother built it." "It's mine now."

She ended the call.

Yes, it was time she changed. Gina realized that too late. She was too good, and people were taking her for granted. Her assistant, Carl had betrayed the trust she had given him and now Fred, had insulted her.

To succeed in her business, she needed to change for good. She would cut off the few people in her life that have negative effects.

Change is the only constant thing in life.

She would need to change the way she dressed and ate. She decided that she was too thin. She needed to add more weight.

"My problem is, I worry too much. I worry about a lot of things that I should have no business worrying about."

She jumped from the bed with a beautiful smile on her face as she got ready to face the next day. She was now a changed person. Changed for good; the only important people in her life were her kids and her best friend Angela.

It was high time she stopped pleasing people and pleased herself. Pleasing herself was her goal because no matter how hard you try to please people, they would still be unappreciative.

"Man can never be pleased."

At her former place of work, when her husband died and she had refused to sleep with colleagues, she was nicknamed "the ice queen."

It didn't matter. She was on her way to becoming a star. Soon, she would be one of California's favorite event planner. People shall seek her out and she shall make a good name for herself. All she needed now was a chef.

Change is the only constant thing in life.

If she didn't change, she would never survive it in the event planning world. She needed to change and starting from now, Gina had promised herself she would never be the same again. She had trusted an accountant too much and he had almost landed her in trouble. The saying that experience is the greatest teacher is indeed true. She had learned, in a very hard way that to survive and excel in her business, change was paramount.

From now, she must change even her calendar and her schedule to accommodate her job. That was the only way to survive. No one and nothing would stop her from achieving her dreams.

Soon, she shall have dozens of clients booking appointments with her.

8

CHAPTER EIGHT

LOYALTY PAYS NO ROYALTIES

Stay true to yourself, yet always be open to learn. Work hard, and never give up on your dreams, even when nobody else believes they can come true but you. These are not clichés but real tools you need no matter what you do in life to stay focused on your path.

-Phillip Sweet

That we find through consistent research is that a lot of people give a lot of loyalty, praise, and homage to things, ideas, people, and beliefs that ultimately do them no good. If anything, it probably causes them more harm than good. They are ready to worry about things that don't really count, things that are worthless. This has ultimately damaged their lives in so many ways you can ever imagine. So, loyalty pays no royalty. Now, I'm not saying that having lack of loyalty in things that you believe in, but there are certain things that we have loyalty in; we have loyalties in beliefs that are self-defeating.

We have loyalties in beliefs that are self-sabotaging, that ultimately set us up for failure. We are very consistent and we're proud in making sure that the world knows that we're loyal to these causes. You take a family, for instance, that came their fifth & sixth generation poor. Instead of someone deciding that it's okay to get a college education, they have this loyal belief that their family is never going to go any further than they have. They are comfortable living with that norm, they believe that it is their lot in life and do little or nothing at all to salvage their situation. Such families end up living in that way until someone decides to put an end to the norm, until someone decides to break the jinx, until someone decides to live above that norm in order to set a new norm. You can never change what you are comfortable with.

Their current station in life is the best that they can aspire to be. It's going to take someone in that family to think outside of that, to have loyalty not just in the family belief

of their limited perspective on life, but to have loyalty in themselves. To say that they are greater than where they're at; that they're capable of doing greater things and can overcome their current situation. See, that is when your loyalty will pay you. But often, the loyalties we have are not paying any type of royalty.

The royalties that are paying, if they are paying your royalties, are a detriment to ourselves. A detriment to our ability, a detriment to our purpose in life, a detriment to our talents and ability to accomplish the things that we want in life. Most people will never understand or even ingest that concept for a couple of reasons: because they are in denial, because they have been conditioned to look at life a certain way, therefore it's hard for them to take an introspective view of themselves, to look at the dynamics of their situation, the dynamics of their family, the dynamics of their whole psychological makeup and conditioning. They're nurtured to say you know what, "what I'm experiencing or what my belief system has been based on is incorrect." So, when they have that limiting belief in themselves, they pay homage, they give loyalty to things that are self-defeating and self-sabotaging. It's no different than a thermostat being set to

60. If the temperature never rises past 60, then it's not going to turn on.

You must correct those belief systems, you must understand that the loyalties you have to things are not going to pay you back with royalties. If anything, they're going to destroy you in the long run. You must make sure that you're

being loyal to the right things that are going to pay you the royalties that you deserve in your life, both professionally and personally.

The second part I want you to understand is that often, we have loyalty to people, individuals, or even sometimes, family members. We have these loyalties to them but the association we have with them ultimately may/will bring us down. I've encountered multiple individuals who have had mental abuse from individuals that were some   of the people they were closest to and they continue, until adulthood, to have issues with certain people.

This means that their loyalty has brought them no royalty. Their loyalty to these people is constantly bringing them down, preventing them from becoming the best person that they can become, it is limiting their belief in themselves, meaning that they can never have self-esteem higher than the thermostat, than the person that they surround themselves with, that they associate themselves with. So whatever that person or individual that's in their life set that thermostat to, that's as far or as high as their expectations of themselves can go. Now, that type of loyalty destroys us because it erodes us from the inside out. It's like an implosion. It starts from the inside and works its way out. It corrupts our entire being and robs us of our joy in life.

Often, it starts when people are children. It can be a parent or a loved one saying that you can't do something because they can't see it for themselves. What you will find out is when someone can't see themselves doing something, they're quick to tell you what you're capable of doing based on

their limitations. They tend to put you under their limitations and judge you by their own weakness. They believe if they cannot do it at age 12, you cannot do it at age 10. They make you believe if they were not able to have that much needed breakthrough, then there is no need to give it a try, you will also end up like them. While you can't control what they say or believe, you can surely control how it gets to you, you can decide to believe them and settle for their limitation or better still prove them wrong. You've got to understand just because that's their limitation does not mean that it's your limitation. We are different. Your limitation can be my strength. The fact that I can't do it doesn't mean you can never be good at it.

You must make sure your loyalty aligns with the best course of action for your life that's going to allow you to be successful, ultimately, and that has nothing to do with everyone else. Everyone else must live their life. Therefore, you must live your life. You must make a decision that will line up with the best possible answer to the equation that comes up with the right product or the right conclusion in your equation. In the end, don't let other people factor into your equation.

Don't let the X carry over in your life. Don't let the unknown of them feed into your equation, which ultimately determines your why. Don't let other people's limitations come over and get into your equation and allow that to be a product of your conclusion, the sum of your beliefs. You cannot allow that to happen. So, understand that we want to pay homage to people that we believe have been influential in our life. We want to pay homage to the beliefs

that we've been brought up on, but at the same time, we must make sure those beliefs and those individuals that we're aligning our loyalty ultimately is a product of our conclusion and allows us to speed line, catapult our lives in the right direction that we would like to see our lives head.

Our life is a ship and we are the only qualified personnel to captain it. There is no way we can captain our ship with the belief of others or wait for them to direct us. We are solely responsible for whatever we believe in. We are accountable only to ourselves and no one else. At the end of the day we will have to sit down to reevaluate our entire existence and we would have woefully failed if we ended up living the life of others. The world has had enough of others, all it needs now is your appearance, it longs to see you in action, it longs to see you take your rightful place, the world patiently awaits your manifestation and you can never do this by judging yourself on the scale of others. You cannot measure the weight of an elephant and an ant on the same instrument. We need to watch our relationships with others, we need to pay special attention to what really counts in our lives. We must really be ready to take the necessary decision on the direction of our lives.

And for whatever reason, if that is not the truth of the situation, then we must distance ourselves away or re- evaluate the relationship and then move forward on what it is that we want to do because ultimately, we're setting ourselves up for failure and we're creating self-sabotage in our own lives through our limiting belief and limiting beliefs

of other people who believe in us. They have limiting beliefs of what we're capable of doing and then it's reaffirmed by us believing, in fact, what they're saying to be true. Watch out for those things. Loyalty pays no royalties.

BRIDGE

The following day was a Saturday. The kids had gone for a sleepover night with their friends and Gina was alone. Her cell phone rang, and she absentmindedly picked it up.

"Good morning girl. How are you and the kids?" She heard Angela's voice from the other side of the line.

"I'm alone. They all went for a sleep over."

"Oh, that's great. How are your plans for the business going?"

"Everything is moving well. In fact, I'm almost through. I've purchase utensils, curtains, chairs, tables and more. I even got two computers for the office."

"I'm so happy for you Gina. I'm glad you're pursuing your dreams."

"I am. I can't work under anyone again. I can't afford to."

"You are braver than I am Gina. I will always respect you for that."

"Thank you."

There was silence for a second or two. "Ken said to tell you hi."

"How is he doing?"

He is fine. He said he has a business meeting. He's getting

ready to leave."

The two friends said their goodbye and ended the call. Gina hung the call and walked upstairs to her room. She peeled off her clothes and filled a tub with hot water.

"I am so tired I need a good soak in the tub."

Gina added bath gel in the water and stepped into the tube.

"Oh God, this is blissful."

She lay down thinking of her business and the unimaginable success it would bring her.

When the water was getting cold, Gina stood up. She washed her hair and left the tub. It was already 8pm when she emerged from the bathroom in a short bathrobe.

Her drenched hair loosely hung around her face. She picked her hand dryer and was about to plug it into a socket when she heard her doorbell rang.

Gina frowned. She wasn't expecting anyone. She wore her slippers and hastily walked downstairs. She pushed the door opened and stared at the tall man standing before her in surprised.

"Hi Georgina?" He called

"Hi Ken, is Angela okay?" She asked, panicking.

"Angela is okay." Ken said. He was dressed in a pair of chinos and evening jacket.

"Please come in."

He entered the room and Gina offered him a seat. "What can I offer you?"

"Oh, I am okay."

"I just got off the phone with your wife. She didn't tell me you were coming."

Ken swept a glance her way. He didn't bother to hide the lust in his eyes. Gina was immediately suspicious.

"Gina, you know you're a beautiful lady, don't you?" "Thanks Kenneth." Was all she could manage to say.

"I've always wanted you. From the first day Angela

introduced you as her friend." Gina took a step backward.

"Get out of my house Kenneth."

He took a step closer. "Who do you think you are? Why are you still mourning a man that is already gone?"

"Get out." She shouted. She felt a twinge of fear at the way he was looking at her.

"When last did you have sex? I know you've always wanted me. I've seen the way you stare at me when you think Angela wasn't watching."

"I don't know what you think you saw. I am not so stupid as to sleep with my best friend's husband."

He reached for her and she tried to dodge but she wasn't fast enough. He picked her up like a piece of paper and threw her on the sofa.

"You are acting all prim and proper when I know you're not." He shouted at her.

Gina scrambled to her feet, but he was on her again, pushing her back into the sofa. Before she could react, he was on her, kissing her and forcing her eyes open. She perceived alcohol in his breath.

Gina couldn't breathe. His hands were on her breasts. She managed to bite him. He jumped and she scrambled to her feet. She didn't wait to see his reaction. She ran upstairs to her room and shut the door.

Two minutes later, she heard him banged the door on his way out. Gina wondered how Angela ended up with a man like Ken. She was crying as she picked her phone and dialed her friend's number.

Angela appeared thirty minutes later. Gina tearfully narrated everything to her.

"You're lying. My husband will never do this."

Gina felt as if she had been slapped in the face. She had never thought her friend would refuse to believe her.

Angela retrieved her phone and called her husband. He appeared in another thirty minutes.

"Did you visit my friend or not?" Angela asked Ken.

"I visited her. I came to check on her and she tried to seduce me."

"That's a lie. You are a great liar." Gina was too surprised.

"Gina I always knew that you wanted my husband. I never knew you would want to destroy my marriage to have him." Angela shouted.

"Angela? You believed him over me? I am your best friend. We've been together for over twenty years and you met him two years ago."

Angela smirked at her friend.

"I don't want to ever see you anywhere near my kids and

I.   Take your husband out of my house and my life."

"Are you sending me away? Aren't you going to apologize?" Angela asked her in shocked.

"If I call you my friend of twenty years and you won't believe me, then there are no need remaining friends with you. Please leave."

Angela stared at her friend. She turned to her husband and they walked away. It wasn't until after she heard their car drove away that she collapsed on the floor and began to cry.

Loyalty is an important thing. It is priceless. There was no need being friends with someone that wouldn't believe her. Twenty years of relationship and her friend had chosen her husband over Gina.

Gina had decided to change for the better last week. She would cut off anything and anyone in her life that would bring nothing good her way. It hurt to cut off her best friend but that would be better.

She felt so betrayed it hurt but she knew that to succeed in life and increase your worth, you would need to know where your loyalty lies and decide. She now knew where her loyalty lay. She had cut off her brother-in-law from her life and now she had just cut off her friend from her life.

"They both don't deserve me." She declared, feeling at peace with herself.

9

CHAPTER NINE

FALSE TENSIONS NEVER CREATE TRUE INTENTIONS

One of the lessons that I grew up with was to always stay true to yourself and never let what somebody else says distracts you from your own goals. And so when I hear about negative and false attacks, I really don't invest any energy in them, because

I know who I am- Michelle Obama.

On January 15, 2018, the whole of Hawaii was sent into a frenzy due to a false alert by authority informing them of an incoming missile attack.

The whole people in Hawaii had to abandon their tasks for the day just to seek shelter from the incoming disaster that was never going to happen. Although this false alert was created as a mistake by a worker, the entire nation was alerted to take the necessary precautions. This false alert created a tension in the whole region that it took the authorities more than 38 minutes to correct the mistake.

This was not true, yet the people had to obey its dictates to stay indoors throughout that day. Now here is the gist, among those held indoors, are people who must have had the day planned out, people who should have been on their way to a business meeting that could change their lives forever, people who should have been on their way to make their life better. All these people were ordered to hide within the comfort of their homes because of an impending danger which will never happen. They were protecting themselves against scenarios that will never come to pass.

Just like the Hawaiian people, a lot of us have gone into hiding due to false tensions which were created by the fear of others. Daily, we tend to listen to statements such as "I don't think you can offer that course in school, we all failed it and you are no way better than us. "Nobody has ever succeeded while doing that kind of business here." "All your siblings never went beyond high school." All these statements are given with an intention to let us know of the already established facts on the ground. From all

these statements and more, we allow our heart to generate false tensions which will never lead us into taking the right decisions.

These individuals took their time to feed our souls with enough lies that we are not ready to move out of that comfort safety zone in order to find out the truth. It is not their faults that they tend to judge us by their own weaknesses, by their own strengths, no. It is our fault that we were ready to subscribe to their truthful lies and allow them to sink deep down into us. I call them truthful lies because these facts are true for them but are lies to you. If you have not failed as they prophesized, then all their facts are false before you.

Life has never been easy, and it will not start with you. From time to time, people are bound to infect you with their negative thoughts on how you ought to live your life, how you ought to plan your entire day, how you can make your life better and all that. Well, one thing they fail to let you know is this; whatsoever works for them may/can never work for you because you are different. You are unique in your own way. While they are done writing their autobiography, you are still in the process of writing yours and unless you apply the full stop, your life can still get better.

These same people will tend to bring you down to the level of their limitations, and give you all the valuable reasons why they believe you can never achieve that goal, you can never get rid of that addiction, you can never have better grades or become what you always wanted to be, and they do all of this from their own point of view.

Once these words are spoken, they sink deep down into your soul and create a false tension which may even lead to an adrenaline rush, you just feel rejected or inspired for a while because they have fueled your passion with lies and hence you just want to act based on these instincts, you just want to relax because your effort will never yield good results, you just want to give up because you have lost the battle even before it started. These false tensions can make you think you cannot be better. It reduces you to the level of a puppet remote controlled by your fears and imprisoned by your negative thoughts.

If you must be a better version of yourself, then you ought to practice the art of selective hearing. Leaders are selective feeders. They don't just subscribe to things people do or say for the fun of it, they go out and gather enough facts and figures to support the motion. This was the same power behind all inventions we see today. Treat people's opinion as invalid unless proven otherwise by your research.

Your false tensions will never give birth to true intentions, false tensions are always leading to false beliefs. False tensions will always lead to forced intentions. Intentions which were induced can be reduced to nothing if we can just take our time to study the ropes and understand why the person is saying what he/she is saying.

Although you are required to be as open as possible to new facts and ideas, it is far better to research on the truth value of the ideas. People tend to tell you their thoughts for one of the following reasons; it is either they want you to be better, to be intimidated or frustrated. Not everyone is

happy about your life and you don't have to live your entire life trying to please others or play their cards. Stop living the life of others. Let your true intentions come from a relaxed and enlightened mind.

You cannot stop them from creating false tensions around you, but you can surely stop these tensions from triggering the wrong fight in your life. Most people have been living their lives fighting off things that never existed simply because a false tension was created around them. These people are hungry for a change of norms; they are ready to change the entire history but are held prisoners by false tensions. The most painful is how they go about neglecting their breakthroughs simply because they were acting on the words of others, leveraging on the experience of others.

Every tension must be brought to the light of the truth, let the truth expose its real nature. Try to gather facts whenever someone is trying to create a false tension in your life. If you know who you really are, no one will be able to challenge you into becoming something you are not meant to be. Remember you are the best version of human the world has ever seen. I have never seen a lion stoop so low as to eat from the grasses simply because it is hungry, no, they are far way better than that.

It is time to move away from that forced intention emanating from the false tension and face the realities of life. One of the fundamental rights of a human is the right to speech, the right to speak whenever they want to. Never get bitter because of their false intentions. Let all your intentions be true.

When you can act out of true intentions, you will never run out of motivation, your life will become easier and your journey lighter. Stop running from things that never exist, stop chasing after shadows.

Before you act on any information, examine what is in for you. Will it end up making you better or worse? Will it lead you to your goals? Does it have the power to change you? After you have established these facts, only then can your intentions be true. Never make decisions while under pressure, never make decisions while in a confused state, make sure you can define your decisions in terms of values and repercussions before going for them.

If they can't do it, disgrace their disbelief by showing them your results. Let your results be your voice. Listen   to them but work out your own ways of having the best intentions. You deserve a better life than this; you deserve to be treated better than this. Never act based on instincts. You are a gift to the world, you have a limited timeline to make the necessary impact, don't waste that time on false tensions, don't waste that time, trying to obey rules that never existed. Your false tensions will never create true intentions. You are who you are unless proven otherwise. Don't let them infect you with their lies; don't let them bring you down to their level, refuse to live within their weakness.

BRIDGE

After the fiasco that led to the betrayal of trust between the two friends, Gina buried herself in her work. She had even opened her office that week and work had begun in earnest. Her assistant was a thirty- five years old woman named Cleo. She was sweet, good and knew a lot. She had experience as an event planner.

Gina had also succeeded in employing a live-in house keeper. The house keeper was a forty- four years old woman. She now took care of the kids and made food for them.

A day before she would pack into her new office, her

neighbor, the owner of the diner had come out to greet her. "Hi, I am Abby." The plump woman introduced.

"Hi, I am Georgina, but you can call me Gina."

They shook hands and Gina decided she loved the woman's smile.

"Your office is beautiful." Abby commented.

"Thanks. Please do tell your friends and acquaintances about us. I will appreciate your patronage."

Abby smiled again, flashing Gina a set of perfect white

teeth.

"Although this is not my business, did you ask around before paying for this office?" She asked Gina, pointing at the office.

"No. Is there a problem?"

"Of course not. Well, if you wouldn't mind me telling you something, I'm sure you haven't heard before."

That got Gina's attention. She looked up at the woman.

"Two years ago, someone committed suicide in that building."

Gina was shocked.

"Are you sure? Are you kidding me?" She asked the woman.

"Of course, I'm not. Everyone knows this."

"What happened? Why would he kill himself?" Gina was

baffled.

"The person that committed suicide was a lady. Rumor has it that she went bankrupt and couldn't bear the shame of it all."

"Oh my God. Poor woman." "That's. Not all."

"There is more?" Gina asked.

"The last person that left the office confirmed that the ghost of the woman that committed suicide is still haunting the place."

Gina almost laughed. She didn't believe in such craps. She was an educated woman. Craps like these would only succeed in weighing someone down.

"You think there is a ghost in my building?" Gina asked.

"Everyone knows that. The last occupant had to leave the building because he couldn't bear it."

"I thought the last occupant moved to Los Angeles.?" Gina couldn't help but to asked.

"Yes. He moved but the ghost sent him away." Gina sighed.

"I don't believe in ghosts. I am an educated woman.

Ghosts don't exist."

"Are you sure?" Abby asked her.

"Yes. When someone dies, the person is gone. There is nothing like a spirit coming back. I don't believe this, and I won't ever believe it."

"Well you should believe this. I don't want to lose you."

Gina looked up at the woman again. They didn't know each other yet she was trying to discourage her from making use of the building.

"You won't lose my dear. I will be fine."

Gina turned to go. It was obvious that the woman was a gossip monger.

"Gina?" Abby called.

"Yes?" Gina said, turning to look at her.

"Due to the fact that there is a ghost in this place, you may not get clients."

"How would you know?" Gina wanted to know.

"I do know. The last occupant lost a lot of clients."

"I will be fine. Please don't worry about me."

She walked away into her office. Cleo, her assistant smiled

when she came in. "Welcome Gina."

"Thank you, Cleo. How are the kids and your husband today?"

"They are all fine, thank you."

From their windowpane, they saw Abby and another woman talking and looking towards them.

"What do you think they are discussing?" Cleo asked. Gina smiled.

"Abby seems to think that there is a ghost lurking around in this part of the building. She said that an occupant committed suicide."

Cleo burst into laughter. She laughed so hard that she held her stomach.

"We are in the twenty first century. How can people think

like this?" Cleo asked her boss.

"This is quite funny. I didn't know people still believed in ghosts until now." Gina supplied.

"They are simply archaic. There is no such thing as ghosts.

They simply don't exist."

"By the way, we need a chef. How about we get one? Do you have one in mind?" Gina asked her assistant.

"Not particular. We can advertise for vacancy."

Gina was determined to not let Abby's opinion ruin her plans to succeed. To success, one needs to shun all negative advice. She knew that she had gotten a good deal with the office and she liked that it was in Beverly Hills. Nothing would discourage her from achieving her goal. No one would stop her from reaching her goal.

She knew that Abby was a gossip. She had just met Gina, yet she had already begun to run her mouth like a tap.

"I don't need people like Abby in my life. They feed on gossips and lies. Wait and see Abby, by this time next year, I will never be the same."

Gina knew that when you listen to what people say, you would end up not getting to your destination. She needed to decide for herself what she should believe in and what she should not. Only then would she survive and then increase her worth. If she should panic at the fact that a ghost lived in her office, she would leave, and her rent would never be returned to her. To Gina, this would be a set back and she didn't want that in her life.

10

CHAPTER TEN

QUANTUM LEAP OR DESPERATE CREEP

"If you must doubt anything, doubt your limits

- Price Pritchett

Maturity has really taught men a great lesson. The more advanced in age you get, the more you realize a lot of things you ought to have done

well, a lot of opportunities you should have accepted, a lot of decisions you should have taken, and the list goes on and on. Age comes with regret and only those who can make the right decisions today can live to enjoy its benefits tomorrow.

Have you ever looked back in time and wondered if a time travel is possible if you could just visit your past for a day in order to correct that wrong that has haunted you for years? Have you ever wished to just have a chance to undo a thing in the past? I am very sure you will draft out a long list of things you will want to be changed from your past. I guess you are not alone in this race; a lot of us had to bite the finger of regret from time to time. Whether we like it or not, there are actions from our past which we regret. To most of us, we feel we should just go back in time to amend our wrongs. If only we could go back in time, we would have accepted that opportunity, we would have tried to prove them wrong, we would have tried to go against our doubts. I can go on and on listing the several regrets that make our past memorable and our present miserable, but the aim of this work will be defeated since it was intended to spur you to success, to become a better version of yourself.

A lot of people who bite the finger of regret today were never opportune to have access to the knowledge you now receive on a platter of gold. You have the power to amend

your future regrets today. If you can do it today, tomorrow will be filled with stories of how your decision assisted you in becoming who you are today. When that happens, you can boldly stand before people and tell them stories about your entire life, stories about how you were able to take that little decision which materialized into the greatest business idea the world has ever known, the greatest invention of the century.

Rather than acting on our dreams, we have successfully put them to sleep by chasing after shadows; we have allowed the mindset of others to control our entire lives, we have left our own lives and have been living to please others. We are more concerned about what they say concerning us than what we think about ourselves. In order to appease them, we have successfully tamed our thoughts and have bent our will to succumb to their wishes. We are ready to give up on our dreams just to make them accept us or feel important in our lives.

One of the greatest challenges of man is not food, shelter or clothing; it is the ability to make valuable decisions. Believe it or not, we are a product of our decisions. You can never be better than your decisions. In life, there is never a thing like indecision. Indecision is also a decision and it is a decision to fail. You cannot sit on the fence, you must take sides. It is either you belong to the doers or the observers. While the doers will never wait for an external source of inspiration, the observers are always seeking approval from friends and family members.

The observers are the category of people who will never lift a finger to help themselves simply because the world has told them they will never succeed. These set of individuals will accept whatsoever the world tells them in good fate and will not give trying a thought. They will never amount to anything or become better. The greatest obstacle to your success as an individual is your decision. Those who suffer from indecision syndrome often end up in the wrong hands. You don't need anybody's approval to make the right decision.

No harm ever came from trying. It is either you are willing to let go of everything to gain something or hold onto everything and receive nothing in return. Before an electron can experience a quantum leap in the atom, it must be able to acquire some charges that move it from the ground state (state of rest) to an excited state (energized state). In the ground state, the electron is simply not charged enough and is at rest. It will continue to be in this position of rest until it is able to acquire new charges and move to the excited state. In the excited state, the electron can exhibit its highest carrying capacity (unleashes its potentials). In this excited state, the electron has received a net charge that can assist it to unleash its potentials to the fullest. The electron at this state of being supercharged will go on to combine with other elements to form compounds (finished products). You will continue to live in your ground state if you don't allow yourself to be energized by an external source of energy. This source of energy comes from you and you alone. No one has the power to make you experience a quantum leap; it is strictly your business and it comes with a confidential tag attached to it.

You owe the world a debt. The solution the world seeks lies in your hands, it is lying helplessly in your brain awaiting manifestation, it is sitting in that dusty bookshelf you have neglected for quite some time now simply because your life is busy. You cannot unleash these potentials of the excited state by dwelling in the ground state; you can never rise to limelight by being comfortable in the ground state. Being energized comes with a price tag. It requires you leaving your comfort zone. It requires your time and sleep, it will demand you to leave that bed and move to the couch, it will require sitting on that chair to draw a blueprint. It will need you to invest your time into learning a new skill. Our beds are too comfortable for our dreams. Your dreams will never see the light of the day if all you do is to sleep all day. Dreamers don't sleep and sleepers never dream. You need to start acting now.

No matter how hard they may seem, your goals are not too high to be reached by you. This is regardless of the how high you set the standards. You have the power to reach them if you are equipped with the right kind of energy. Rather than creeping to achieve your goals, you can easily leap and get a hold of them.

Do you know that if you don't guide the choices you make today, you will wake up tomorrow and wished you had done something better with your today? Make today count by engaging in only the things that make your tomorrow shine. Have you ever imagined how useless that certificate?

will turn out to be simply because you never took the time to plan well? Have you ever thought of how miserable your life will look like after chasing shadows for a very long time? I guess you haven't given that much of a thought. You will end up regretting every bit of your decision if you fail to prioritize and act when necessary.

Never allow your limits to become your limitations. The sky is wide enough to accommodate every flying creature. While some fly at moderate heights there are those who fly at very great heights. The average fliers will never refuse to fly simply because there is another bird which flies higher. Rather than being limited by your limitations, you can turn them into great avenues to lift you up. You don't have to creep when you can leap. Leave your ground state, leave your comfort zone, acquire the right kind of charges and move to the next level.

You can't acquire the right charges when you are glued to the wrong people or source. You can't have a quantum leap while resisting the power of change. You can't be energized if all you agree to feed on is nothing, but the lies spoken from the lip of others who are finding a way to limit you. Your limits should not be used to set your standards, if you are interested in moving forward, you must be ready to let go of your present position. You must be absent to be present. You can't be existing in the ground state and expect to have access to the benefits attached to dwelling in the excited state.

The choice to make the right decision to avoid biting the

finger of regret when tomorrow comes can be avoided today.

Kindly make a choice from this; which will you choose? A quantum leap or a desperate creep?

BRIDGE

Gina was the only daughter of her parents. Her father was a Cardiologist while her mother was a Liberian. She grew up in a suburb of Boston. As an only child, she had all the things money could buy. Her parents were very dotting and made sure she had everything. She was happy, contented and at peace.

When she was six, her father bought a cabin. They often go to the cabin during summers. She often went fishing with her father while her mother prepared dinner.

Gina was so close to her father that she sometimes fell ill when he went on business trips. It was her father that had taught her how to fish. It was he that had taught her swimming and skipping. She had everything she would ever need.

When she was ten, her parents dropped her off at school. It was her Father's Day off at the hospital. When school closed, she had waited in vain for her mother to come for her. Thirty minutes later, Gina was already angry with her parents for forgetting her.

"They had never forgotten me." She kept saying.

By evening, a car drove into the school. Two cops alighted from the car. They stared hard at her and then asked her to show them the headmistress office.

Gina pointed at the woman's office. She was anxious for either of Gina's parents to come for her. After about five minutes, the headmistress walked to Gina.

"Sweetheart come, here." Gina innocently walked to her.

The woman went on her knees in front of her. "Sweetheart, I'm sure you are angry with your mom for

being late."

"Yes." She said in a small tone.

"You know your mother is never late, don't you?" "Why is she late today? Please call her."

"I tried calling her Gina, she wasn't picking up."

"Call my dad. He will pick up. He would be home." She said.

"I'm so sorry sweetheart, I have got some bad news for you" the woman said.

"What is it? Are the cops taking me home?"

"Yes Gina. You see, after your parents dropped you off at school this morning, they were involved in an accident."

"Are they going to be alright?" Gina desperately asked.

"Sweetheart, your parents had both gone to heaven."

For a minute, Gina didn't understand what the woman meant. Slowly, her words sunk in. Gina went cold. She

fainted in sheer shock.

When she opened her eyes, she was already at home. She cried her eyes out. Her parents had no living relatives. The burial was a very small one. Gina knew her life would never be the same again.

Social services came for her immediately after the burial. "I don't want to leave." She sobbed.

"Of course, you have to."

Two weeks later, Gina was taken to a foster home in another suburb. It was never home. She missed her parents. Although she was living with his parents, Davis had been the best brother she would have asked for. They became close. He was two years older than she was.

Gina met Angela in school. She was also in a foster care home. The three grew up together. After high school, Gina went to study event planning.

Davis was very supportive. She had since lost her father's fortune. Their house couldn't cover insurance and it was taken from her.

After graduation, Gina made her first hard decision. She decided to study accounting. Her foster parents wouldn't allow her. She went for evening classes and worked in the afternoon.

Davis stood by her the whole time. She was twenty when he asked her to marry him. Although they both had their fair share of relationships, they had always been secretly in love.

His parents refused to approve of her. His brother, Fred had also refused. Davis had gone against their wish and had married her in a very small church with Angela serving as her chief bridesmaid. Their marriage cost him his family. His parents stopped talking to him.

"I love you Gina, there is peace in this feeling."

When he died in an auto accident, Gina finally came   to realize that God didn't want her to be happy. First her parents had died and then her husband. The only things that had kept her going were her kids.

Today, although she was fully healed, she sometimes missed him. He was the only one who had truly loved her unconditionally apart from her parents.

"It is high time I start dating."

Gina finally decided.

She was standing by her window staring down the street. She didn't want her kids to grow up without a father. She knew this was a decision she must make.

"Can I really fall in love again?" She wondered.

She decided to quit her job of six years; she had also decided to increase her worth by starting her own business. She decided to think of her life and planned to cut out some toxic people who didn't need to be in her life. It hurt that Angela didn't believe her, but she knew it was one of the hardest decisions she had taken.

Finally, Gina decided to fall in love again, marry a man that would love her and her kids unconditionally. She needed a man that would support her and help her grow. Any man that would bring about negative change in her life was a no. She needed a man that would put smiles on her face and the face of her kids.

In business, the ability to decide and stand firmly by it is important. She knew that it wouldn't be easy, but she was tired of men coming after her. After all, no one wants to be alone. She smiled, knowing that her life was finally taking the right shape.

11

CHAPTER ELEVEN

THINGS OF FASHION OR THINGS OF PASSION; IT ALL DEPENDS ON YOUR REACTION

Every great dream begins with a dreamer. Always remember, you have within you the strength, the patience, and the passion to reach for the stars to change the world

- Harriet Tubman

L ife is all about interests, where your interest lies determine where your strength goes to. People don't tend to engage in things their minds are not settled with. If you are the type who is bothered by the outlook of things, then you will end up spending several days and nights worrying about appearances. If you are the type that bothers only about the things that make you happy, you will surely stay up even at night to find a way of birthing them.

Dreaming is good; it is good that all men dream. A dream is as good as useless unless someone decides to act on it. Dreams need the mindset of achievers before they can materialize. While achievers can go the extra mile to bring a dream to life, dreamers tend to go back to sleep. A dreamer is not better than a loser, they both have something in common; they lack results. They lack valuable results to show for all the work they've engaged in, they lack tangible results to show for everything they stand for. They are not even result oriented.

Man needs knowledge and priorities. Man requires knowledge of how several things should be done. Without knowledge, we will end up living our lives defeated and without purpose. Remember we said you are a gift to the world; remember we said you owe the world a great debt. These debts can only be repaid through your contribution to the world. You are a part of the bigger picture that sees the problem and wants to solve it. You are unique in your own way. Your contributions to the world can only come from you.

We need to learn how to react to things in different situations. We need to learn how to give each situation the best reaction. Things that do not matter should be treated with little or no seriousness while things that really matter should be treated with great attention. Amongst things that really matter, we also need to pay special attention to those that require an urgent response from us. We need to learn the act of giving our tasks preferences. Before engaging in a task, we need to ask ourselves these questions. Is this task important? Why should I engage in this task? What are the short and long-term benefits of engaging in this task? What are the repercussions of not engaging in these tasks? Does this task have a timeline? Can I do it later? What if I fail to do it now, am I likely to suffer consequences?

Spend time to work on the things you are passionate about, spend enough time to invest in the things your heart longs for. These are the things that are supposed to give you a relaxed mind; these are the things that comfort you when everyone is away. Never treat your passion with carelessness, never allow your present situation to rob you of the joy of enjoying the bliss of tomorrow. If you are passionate about some things, go for those things, hold onto them and treat them with all seriousness.

Today only comes once in a lifetime. If you fail to do what you are expected today, you will surely spend the whole of tomorrow paying the debts of today. Stop using today to pay for yesterday's debt.

There is a need to also pay special attention to appearances because they can be deceiving. Several people have rejected the opportunities of becoming great just because success came to them wearing an overall. The fact that it appears messy does not mean the result will be useless besides, raw materials are always looking dirty compared to their finished products. Make out time to change your raw materials into results, be patient enough to work on your materials, the world is only interested in your success. The world will never remember the man that came second, it only celebrates winners.

Clearly define where your interest in life lies, set down goals and never compromise on them. Never ever lower your standards for anybody. People should be able to accept you for who you are, they should accept you just as you are. Unless you have a bad character such as addictions and wrong approaches to life, people should not try to change you. Let people know who you truly are and accept you for that.

Be open to change. Only those who can accept change can become great. Greatness is in every man, it dwells in you. Be ready to let go, let go of that bad habit, let go of that wrong motive, let go of all the bitterness in life, let go of anything that cannot add value to your life. Let go and accept change.

Never believe you are a loser, you can never be a loser.

You won your first battle on the day you were conceived.

You were born a winner. Never allow anyone make you think less of yourself. If anybody can do it, then it must be you. If anyone can provide the solution, it must be you. You are a gift to the world.

Your reaction to things will give them a true meaning in life. What you look at, determines your position in life. Chase after passion, run after it, and fashion will be delivered to you as a full package. Channel your strength to do what matters the most. You can only be remembered for one thing; the problems you created or solved. Where do you belong? Are you a part of the solution or problem? I want you to think deeply on this. Your reaction determines where your strength goes to.

BRIDGE

Gina was yawning. It had been two weeks and she was yet to get a single client. She promised herself to not give up. She stretched her hands against the oak table in front of her. She had already advertised her business online, the daily times and even through chat rooms. All she needed now were customers.

"No, I won't give up."

She heard her assistant phone began to beep. Later, her land line rung, and Gina reached for it.

"Gina, there is a man who would love to talk with you." She heard her assistant's voice.

Gina's heart leapt with joy.

"Please patch us through."

A few seconds later, she heard a deep male voice spoke from the other end of the line.

"Good morning. Am I speaking with Miss Georgina Davis?"

"Oh yes. How may I be of help?"

"My name is Abram. I need an event planner." Gina beamed.

"You've reached the right person."

"I'm getting married in three weeks. I saw your ad online and I managed to go through your site."

"Thank you, Mr. Abram."

"I think it would be good if my fiancée and I come over to your office."

"That would be a great idea."

"How much do you charge?" He asked.

"Well, it depends on what you want exactly. When we meet, we can talk it over."

"You're probably right." After a short pause, the man said, "I will keep in touch. Do have a wonderful day Miss Davis."

"You too."

The line went dead. Gina's assistant Cleo knocked on the door and poked her head into the room.

"Did we just have our first client?"

Gina beamed.

"I think so. He would be here with his fiancée tomorrow

morning. Goodness Cleo, I am excited."

"Don't worry Gina. You've worked hard for this. You shall get this job and many more."

"Amen."

The women laughed.

The following day, Gina had just bid her first client a

farewell and she felt so happy.

"We made it." She shouted at Cleo.

The women smiled. She returned to her office to begin

planning when her phone beeped.

"There is a man here to see you Gina. He is a Chef. He said he has an appointment."

"Oh yes, I totally forgot. Please send him in." "Okay."

Two minutes later, Gina heard a knock on her door. She bides him to enter and stood up to welcome him. For the first time in ages, her heart missed a beat. She stared hard at the man before her. He was dressed in a black suit. On his

feet were a pair of oxfords. She looked at his face. He was handsome-no, not handsome, he was beautiful. His brown hair was cut low. His eyes were blue-as blue as the deep blue sea. For some reason, he smiled, and Gina almost smiled back.

He had the perfect set of teeth she had ever seen. His pink lips were full and tempting. They seemed to be calling her. She allowed her gaze to move down his body. He had broad shoulders and lean body. He wasn't just sexy; he had the body of an athlete. He was obviously spending a lot of time at the gym. At six feet, he was very tall.

"Good morning Miss Davis. I am Harrison Hughes." He said stretching his hands.

Gina took his hands and almost bolted. For the first time since her husband died, she felt butterflies at the bottom of her stomach.

"It is nice meeting you Mr. Hughes. Please have a seat."

He did and the two stared at each other. The two had been talking on the phone. She never realized he was so cute.

"Tell me about yourself."

"I am Harrison Hughes. I am 32 years old. I graduated from the culinary institute of America, Hyde Park. I have a degree in associate of Occupational Studies-Baking and pastry arts. I..."

Gina waved her hands away.

After another thirty minutes, she hired the man. He

walked out of the office and she felt like a schoolgirl again.

She was about to leave the office when Angela rushed into her office in tears.

"Gina, I am so sorry I didn't believe you." "What happened?"

"I caught him cheating on me on our matrimonial bed."

Gina held out her hands and her friend walked into them.

She was crying her eyes out.

"Don't cry over him sweetie. He doesn't deserve you." "I feel so very stupid."

"Tell me, are you pregnant?" She asked her friend. "No, I'm not."

"It is now your decision to make. Choose whether you want to stay with him or leave."

"I can't stay with him. I have to leave." "Are you sure?"

"Yes."

Exactly one month later, Gina was at her window. She saw Harrison walked into the building. She knew she was in love. She had never felt this alive in her life. Sometimes, she caught him staring at her when he thought she wasn't looking.

"Is he also attracted to me?" She asked out loud. A loud knock came at her door.

"Come in." She said.

The door came opened and the man that had haunted her nights strolled in.

"Good morning Miss Gina."

"Good morning Harrison." Do you need something?" "Yes."

He walked towards her and Gina's heart began to beat faster. H stepped a foot away from her.

"Miss Gina, I can't work for you anymore." "Why?" She was surprised.

"I am attracted to you Gina. I can't work with you and yet not be able to touch you."

Gina was on him. She joined her lips with his and they kissed very passionately.

"I love you Harrison. I've always loved you. From that

day you walked into this office and..."

He captured her lips again.

"Can we give it a try?" He asked her a few minutes later. "I have two kids, I once..."

He placed his finger on her lips.

"I know that sweet but that doesn't change how I feel about you."

Her phone began to ring. She knew she was finally where she wanted to be. She was now fulfilled. Her business was thriving, her kids were happy and now she had found love again. What else would she want? She had gone for what she wanted, and she was happy. She had now realized that she had passion for event planning.

"No day of our lives shall ever be boring." He promised her.

Gina smiled and burrowed closer to him. She was glad she had followed her heart. She knew a new chapter was about to be written in her life. Her happiness had always been in her hands and she never realized it until now.

CONCLUSION

DO IT NOW

You are not short of great ideas, you are not unskilled, you are not inferior, forget about all the lies you've been told concerning your life, their rules of failure and success doesn't apply to you, you are not weak, you are not useless, you are the greatest gift the world has ever received, you are the best of your kind, the only solution to the problems in the world. You are a great man or women with a little challenge and once you can overcome, the sky will be your starting point. In all these accolades, you lack just a single thing. It is a friendly enemy which gives you false hope and creates a false tension in your life. What you lack is the ability to act on the things that matter most.

Your inability to identify things that really matter and require your urgent attention will send you on an errand to the land of failure. Stop majoring on the minors because they are called "minors" for a reason.

Never dedicate your time to doing things that will never make you better. Disconnect yourself from any form of wrong association, never allow bitter and negative people to get the better part of you. Never give them a chance to imprison you, never allow them to look down on your dreams, never give them the opportunity to judge on their scales, and never allow them to make you believe in their weaknesses.

If you have a dream, act on it now, follow your passion and never look back, don't build or write your life's story with the pen of others. Your dreams come with an expiry date, if you must act on them, the time is now. Never allow procrastination to rob of your joy. Everyone has a right to live his or her life. No one will ever reward you for being a zombie.

As I bring this book to a close, I challenge you to do it now. I challenge you to have a dream, work on that dream, make that dream a reality and save the world. Run until you achieve your goals, run until you can catch your vision, run until your status changes, run until the negative people can no longer have a hold on you, run until you are able to succeed. Everything is possible if you can believe in yourself, the power of your vision and skills. Life is too short to focus on things that don't matter.

Reading this book is not enough. It would be a total waste of time to read through and still wait for permission to start engaging in the things that makes you happy. Start your journey now. All you need to succeed has been made available to you. Utilize it properly. Cheers!

ABOUT THE AUTHOR

Brandon L. Draper is a serial entrepreneur, best-selling author, transformational business coach, and TV & Radio host. He is recognized as a person of leadership, negotiations and organizational turnaround, he has served as an advisor to innovators, small business owners, fortune 500 companies, any many more around the world for more than 15 years. The author wrote this book for business owners and entrepreneurs looking for a slight edge or ideas to take their business to the next level. The author Brandon L. Draper, better known as the Motivational King is an Amazon bestselling author, international speaker, business innovator, social media personality and top leadership development trainer featured in many news publications around the country.

Want to Attend One of Our

FREE Write Publish & Profit Workshops?

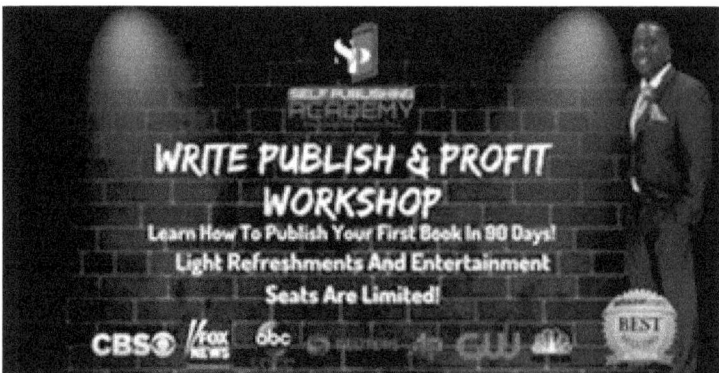

Visit Us At

www.SelfPublishCentral.com/events Featured Locations

- Atlanta GA
- Los Angeles California
- Washington DC
- Miami Florida
- More Cities to Come!

Get Your Write Publish & Profit

Workbooks

Book Creation Workbook

Virtual Book Tour Workbook

Book Signing Workbook

Book Bestseller Workbook

Get Your Workbooks Today!

http://bit.ly/2RIRWHM

Sign Up for The Self- Publishing Academy

Learn how write and publish your

first or next book to generate new clients,

lead generation or to get speaking engagements.

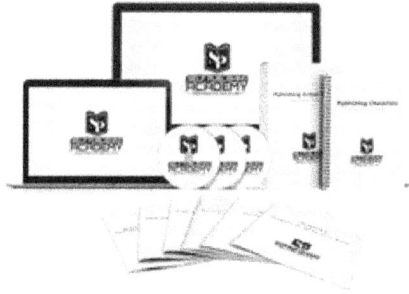

Normally $1,997.00

FINAL PRICE:

$297.00

ENROLL BELOW

http://bit.ly/2sGhlmq